Small Spaces
for modern living

Small Spaces
for modern living

making the most of your indoor space

Caroline Atkins

hamlyn

First published in Great Britain in 2003 by

Hamlyn, a division of Octopus Publishing Group Ltd

2–4 Heron Quays, London E14 4JP

Copyright © Octopus Publishing Group Ltd 2003

Distributed in the United States and Canada by

Sterling Publishing Co., Inc.

387 Park Avenue South, New York, NY 10016-8810

ISBN 0 600 60955 3

A CIP catalogue record for this book is available from the British Library

Printed and bound in China

10 9 8 7 6 5 4 3 2 1

contents

introduction

Gauging and using space effectively is one of the most important elements of design – the less space you have, the more deftly it needs to be handled. To create a room that is aesthetically pleasing as well as practical and comfortable, you need to be sensitive to the proportions of the space available, aware of the sightlines and focal points you are establishing and sure about the effect you want to achieve. Space does not exist purely to be filled up with furniture and fittings: it is the oxygen that lets the room breathe. It has its own value and this must be respected if you want to make the most of it. Remembering this is particularly crucial in modern design, which is as much about what you leave out as what you put in. Empty spaces are just as eloquent as the furnishings they surround, giving each room essential accents and highlights, like punctuation marks in a sentence, and providing variety of pace alongside furniture and artefacts.

But it can be hard to approach space objectively – and especially hard to restrain yourself from grabbing at every spare bit of it – when it is in relatively short supply. Most of us would like more space in our homes, either for practical use or simply to provide a more open, airy setting for our possessions. The principle behind this book is to help you make the most of whatever space you have – however limited it seems at the outset – and encourage it to work in your favour rather than seeing it as a constant source of frustration.

The following chapters will help you to create more space in your home, both practically by guiding you through sensible storage and clutter-control decisions, and visually by showing you how clever choices of style and colour can open up the rooms around you. They will also help you to see the benefits that small spaces can offer by showing you how to capitalize on the sense of warmth and intimacy conjured up by a more enclosed atmosphere. Whether you want to change the effect of your space or exploit its confined nature for the best, this book will provide all the advice and information you need.

The first two chapters lay down the ground rules, outlining the design principles you need to bear in mind when dealing with small spaces, and working through the decisions you have to make about the home you want to create. There are essential questions for you to ask yourself about your lifestyle, family and furnishing preferences, and basic options to consider before you launch into the decorating itself. Do you want clearly defined rooms or an open-plan living space? Which activities are most important to you – cooking and entertaining, or relaxing and watching television? How much time will you spend in each area? And how many people will need to use them at once? All these concerns need to be taken into account in order to build up a clear picture of the home you want.

The book then devotes a chapter to each room in turn, and guides you through the process of choosing colours, lighting, furniture, flooring and accessories, highlighting potential pitfalls, suggesting space-making solutions and identifying key pointers for clutter control. At the end of each chapter you will find one or two 'room recipes', which break down room schemes into their constituent ingredients and demonstrate how you can make them work together to create highly effective small spaces for modern living.

opposite *Light colours and clean surfaces create a sleek, modern space for living, cooking and eating – combining varied activities in a single open-plan area.*

below *Natural brickwork adds a strong industrial look that provides an appropriate backing for simple furnishings and functional materials.*

7

Wanting more space has become a mantra for our time, as though space were a necessity rather than a preference. But the only way to make it work successfully is to know *why* you want it, and in order to do that, you have to start prioritizing. What space is currently available and how do you use it? Where would you like more space and where could you manage with less? Which is more important to you: storage space for personal possessions or living space for family and friends?

The secret to creating extra space is getting to know your home and thinking practically about your lifestyle, then putting the two together and seeing what compromises and adjustments need to be made. Take it slowly and do not act on a whim: short-term wants may not fulfil long-term needs, and decorating a house – even a small one – is a long-term investment.

Be guided by the style of the architecture, but do not let it dictate to you. The fact that a building is old, for instance, does not prohibit you from decorating the space in a modern style. The beauty of period buildings is their individuality. Elegant lines, interesting architectural details – even uneven walls – all contribute their own natural character, and keeping your decoration and furnishings clean and contemporary is one of the most effective ways to enhance them. Concentrate on the space, not the façade or interior fittings. Doors and fireplaces can always be removed or replaced, walls and stairs moved or remodelled, but the space is yours, so make sure that it works for you.

1 PLANNING & PRIORITIZING

assessing your lifestyle

However much space you have, it can easily be wasted if you do not know what to do with it. So before you think about decorating and furnishing, consider how you are going to live in it. That way, you can reclaim space where it is not important and redistribute it where you need it.

Think about how you spend most of your time: cooking? entertaining? watching television? reading? working? Or have you got hobbies that need space: painting, engine-stripping or playing an instrument? If you are a single person who never takes work home, usually eats out and has an unhealthy obsession with pool, then a games room – or a huge living room – is probably more

use to you than a study or a large kitchen. On the other hand, if you have school-age children and enjoy having friends to dinner, plenty of kitchen space and somewhere for homework become urgent priorities.

LIFESTYLE QUESTIONS

Start by asking yourself a few basic questions about your lifestyle, so you can be sure that you are planning for your own particular needs.

Have you any children?

The answer to this question will influence how you distribute your space and decorate it. Sleeping space is the first consideration: do they need separate rooms or can they share? Children usually draw the short straw when it comes to handing out bedrooms, but if they are prepared to share, it could be worth giving them the biggest room and freeing up the smallest for a study. You should also consider their schoolwork and extra-curricular activities. These will vary according to age, but at different stages you are likely to need space for toys, homework, music practice, teenage rock groups and sleepovers. If this space is not provided by their bedrooms, you will have to create it in other areas, and these will need furnishing in a robust style: white sofas and cream carpets may not be practical.

Do you work from home?

If you are a full-time home-worker, you already know how much space it takes up, and this should be a priority when you are allocating rooms. If you are also part of a busy household, you will probably need to find a dedicated space that can be closed off for quiet and privacy. If you have the place entirely to yourself, you may prefer to create a work area in the main living space. Anyone who takes work home will appreciate a study if there is room for it, but unless it is a priority, you will probably have to make do with a corner of the living room.

below *Finding space for your possessions means balancing storage and display. Here, books, pictures and other artefacts are mixed together on open shelves that have been fitted neatly under the slope of the ceiling to make the most of the difficult wall space.*

How much do you cook or entertain?

Which activity is more important to you? Is it plenty of room to cook for your family and friends, or enough space to enjoy eating with them? Considering this question will help you decide whether you need a full-sized kitchen for food preparation or whether you are better off limiting it to a neat run of cabinets and reallocating the rest of the space as a dining room. It may be that you do not need a separate kitchen at all, but could create a galley area at one end of a large living space.

Do you need space for overnight guests?

It is surprising how many homes include a spare room that is kept like a shrine in a permanent state of waiting for someone to come and stay. If your spare room is not occupied for more than a few nights a year, it could be put to better use as a study or playroom. You do not need to shun guests altogether: equip the space with a sofabed, which can provide sleeping space at short notice, and you will simply be getting double value out of a single room.

Are you a hoarder or a minimalist?

Minimalists are so tidy by nature that they do not actually need much space to accommodate them. Hoarders will have to work much harder to find space for all their things, and will need to devise ingenious storage systems. If you are a hoarder, you might consider designating one room for most of your possessions, so that you can keep the main living areas spacious and free from clutter.

By working through these questions, you should be able to establish your space-making priorities and gauge whether you need more sleeping space or room for entertaining, whether the kitchen needs space for cooking or for eating and whether the sitting room needs to house a

dining table, too. You will know how much space you need for a television and other home-entertainment equipment and whether you are likely to need hidden cupboard space rather than open display shelves. Now you need to work out whether the space you have available works as it is, or whether it needs rearranging to suit the way in which you plan to use it.

below *Reflective surfaces and fitted furniture increase the sense of space in a compact kitchen and contribute a stark, professional edge to the style of the room.*

PRIVATE SPACE OR OPEN-PLAN LIVING?

The idea of open-plan spaces is sometimes more attractive than the reality. They look wonderful in books and magazines, but before you decide to knock down walls and run rooms into one another, think about the privacy you will be losing by not being able to close the door on clutter. Will you be disciplined enough to keep the whole space in order, and will you miss the comforting cosiness provided by smaller, enclosed rooms?

assessing your space

Every building is different. Its shape, size, age and architecture give it a distinctive character that needs to be taken into account when you are planning how to use it.

Give yourself time to get to know your home before you start imposing your design plans on it. This usually means waiting for a few weeks after you move in (or preferably a couple of months) while you feel your way around.

Establish which rooms feel most comfortable at different times of day – which are the lightest, which are quietest, which have the best views and which are overlooked? Trust your instincts and take note of which spaces you tend to avoid and which you gravitate towards. Consider how you can make the most of your preferred areas, and think about the other parts that need to be rearranged in order to create more usable space, perhaps by moving doorways or knocking rooms through into one another.

Try to forget the existing furnishings and instead look for the potential of the space. Do not be put off by unsympathetic wall colours and shabby carpets, and learn to distinguish between permanent fixtures and things that can be changed. Built-in storage is useful, but can be removed if it is not needed, and it may be much more effective somewhere else instead.

ESTABLISHING YOUR BOUNDARIES

The important thing at this stage is to establish exactly what room you have got to play with so that you can make the most of its potential. Do not be disheartened by an apparent lack of space: knowing your boundaries is the first step towards being able to work constructively within them. With a house or apartment, you need to be able to imagine the outline clearly before you can work out exactly how to use the space within it and start building up your own picture of colours and furnishings.

It is also important to bear in mind that having too much space can be as problematic as having too little. Deciding how to furnish a cavernous warehouse is daunting because you do not know where to start. Having a clearly defined space from the outset will help you make initial design decisions by reducing the options so that you have fewer choices to make.

GETTING STARTED

How clearly you can see the outline of your space depends partly on whether the house is new to you or all too familiar. Have you just moved in, full of plans, knowing the space is limited but inspired by good intentions to make the most of it? If so, then you are seeing it with fresh eyes and clear sight, unjaded by experience. However, you do not know it well enough to envisage how you will live in it, how the space works, where the light falls, how that awkward door opens the wrong way and blocks the corridor… Give yourself time to get used to your

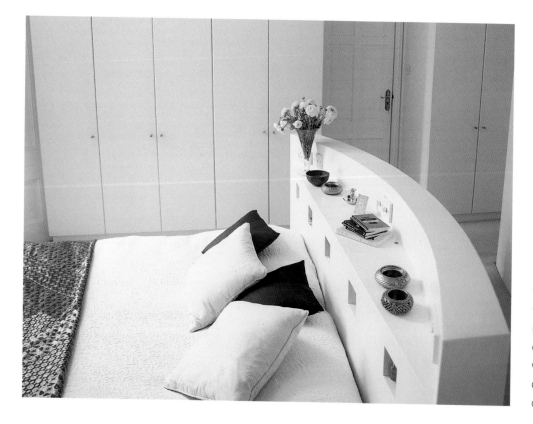

below *A free-standing headboard for your bed provides you with ample extra storage and display space, as well as creating a screen that helps to keep your sleeping space separate from the dressing and clothes storage areas.*

design options:

left *Slotting storage crates under tables will provide extra space without disrupting the low furnishing lines.*

below *High-level shelves fitted into recesses and above doorways will let you display personal possessions and store less regularly used items out of the way while leaving valuable floor space clear.*

POINTS TO CONSIDER

Get to know the building thoroughly before you make any major design decisions. Ask yourself these questions:

- Which direction does it face?
- Which rooms face the road/overlook the garden/have other views?
- Which rooms get most light at which times of day?
- Which rooms are the quietest?
- Which rooms have the most wall and floor space?
- Which rooms have the highest ceilings?
- Do any rooms lead into one another?
- Are there any wasted corners or unusable spaces?
- Are there any doors that open awkwardly?
- Are there any narrow corridors causing obstructions?
- Are there any doorways or corners that make furniture access unnecessarily difficult?
- Which walls are structurally supporting and which are partitions?

new home, to get a feel for how you will live in it. Do not rush straight in with your most ambitious and imaginative plans.

Or is it somewhere you have lived for some time and grown too big for? Has it filled up until you cannot see the edges and have no space to turn round? If so, you will know all the problems and be aware of which rooms are most comfortable at which time of day. But you are probably bogged down with clutter and frustration, and are unable to see it in a new light. Take a step back and envisage it without its over-abundant contents.

TURNING SPACE UPSIDE DOWN

The convention of living downstairs and sleeping above no longer makes sense when you consider that it is the upper rooms that tend to get the most daylight and that these are wasted by being used solely at night. Take a look at many new house designs and you will find that they are turning this style of living upside down, with bedrooms downstairs and living space on the upper floors to take full advantage of the light. It could be worth rethinking your layout to turn the bedrooms into daytime living space.

A BLANK CANVAS

Depending on your budget and timetable, it can be useful to paint the entire space white or off-white so that you have a blank canvas to start with. In fact, it may save you both time and money in the long run if it prevents you making expensive mistakes. Neutral and space-enhancing, white will highlight the shape of the space, defining its lines and opening up dark corners and awkward angles. It will help you to see the space for what it is, and will be easy to live with until you make more definite design decisions.

assessing the possibilities

Having established what you need and how much space is available, compare the two to assess how closely they coincide and what adjustments are needed to balance them. You need to distinguish between genuine needs and more superficial wants, and probably make a few sacrifices to make the most effective use of the space you have.

Make a list of all the activities and items you want to make space for – cooking, eating, entertaining, office work, creative work, relaxing, playing games, playing musical instruments, exercising. Now divide this list into two: a 'must have' list for the absolute essentials and a 'would like' list for the things you want space for if at all possible. This may seem obvious, but it is a very subjective process and will throw up surprising variations from one person to another. You are the only one who knows whether or not you can live without your piano or multigym, and how many people you need to fit regularly round your dining table. Be sure to consult all members of the household to get their views, too.

If you cannot decide which list a particular item belongs in, give it a mark out of five, where five equals maximum need. Relegate anything scoring three or less to the wants list and use as reserves to be slotted in if there is room later.

Now apply the same principle to the design changes that you are thinking of making, from open-plan living to requisitioning the spare room. Most decisions will have two sides to them, so consider carefully whether the benefits outweigh the disadvantages, and then give them a score out of five according to how badly you want to make the change.

RADICAL RETHINKS

Some of the decisions will make themselves for you without much difficulty; others need more thinking through. The key choices are whether or not you need to radically rethink the kitchen and bathroom. These are the rooms where plumbing,

electricity and construction will be most labour-intensive and expensive, so they should become priorities if you want to make major changes.

First, are they where you want them? Does the position make sense? Is the bathroom close to the rooms that you are planning to use as bedrooms? Is the kitchen within easy reach of your dining area? Now think about their size.

design options:

WEIGHING UP PROS AND CONS

- Knocking down walls gives you more space and light but less privacy and less room to hang pictures.
- Reversing upper and lower floors makes living spaces lighter but may involve sleeping on the ground floor, which some people are not comfortable with.
- Incorporating the kitchen into the living area reclaims wasted cooking space but means that there is no door to hide cooking smells or unwashed dishes.
- Dedicating the spare room to work space or personal clutter keeps the rest of your living area clear but it means that you do not automatically have overnight space for guests.

opposite *Half-height walls and an interior framework can create rooms within rooms to demarcate your space. Expansive windows and wood floors and ceilings add an industrial, warehouse-style look.*

above *Where space is limited, furniture needs to be chosen carefully. Streamlined curves and practical folding designs are invaluable, and built-in storage will hide clutter behind a neat wall of closed doors.*

Is the bathroom too small? Would you rather convert one of the bedrooms into a decent-sized bathroom and use the existing one as a utility room? Or is it unnecessarily large? Would you prefer to swap the luxurious bath for a smaller shower room and use the wasted space to create a useful office area?

PRACTICAL RESTRICTIONS

Now make a list of all the other factors that are likely to restrict what you can and cannot do. How big is your budget for furnishings, decorating and any restructuring work needed on top of that? You will not be able to calculate the last of these costs exactly until you have consulted builders and, if necessary, architects. However, you can take it for granted that it will be more than you expect, so bear this in mind before you set your heart on grand plans.

Be prepared to scale your ideas down and settle for a few cheaper options and improvisations.

How much of the work will you be able to tackle yourself and which jobs will need professional help? And how much upheaval can you cope with? You cannot predict with any certainty whether doing the work yourself will be less disruptive than paying someone else. If you are doing it, it will take longer and you will probably hit stressful periods of panic and despair. If it is someone else, you will have to cope with sharing your house with them, so think it through and decide which route will cause you fewer sleepless nights and family rows.

All these factors – the way you live, the space you want, the raw materials you are starting with and the budget you are working within – need to be weighed up and balanced in order to establish just what is possible for you to achieve.

using the space

Before you start to put any of your plans into action, you will need to back up your assessment of the space you have with some accurate dimensions. Then you can create an accurate scale plan and start work.

Measure all the relevant distances in your home, including the width of corridors, the width and height of doorways, the space between windows and each room's ceiling height, as well as its length and width. These measurements will allow you to create a floor plan drawn to scale. Start with an overall plan of the space (or a plan for each floor if you have more than one) so that you can see how the rooms fit together and allocate areas of use, then draw up separate plans as you progress to individual rooms.

MAKING A FLOOR PLAN

This procedure can be followed each time you plan a new room. For each plan, use squared or graph paper and a scale of around 2.5cm (1in) to represent 1m (3ft). Mark all fixed features such as doors, windows, alcoves and fireplaces with 'semi-fixed' items such as radiators and power points marked in a different colour. It is helpful to know where these are, but they should not over-influence your plans as they can be moved in most cases.

Mark on the plan which areas you are designating for different uses and different times of day, and start thinking about essential furniture – kitchen cupboards, beds, tables.

left *Fitting the kitchen into the corner of an area keeps appliances out of the way and leaves the main floor clear for living space. Adding flashes of bright colour prevents the predominantly white scheme from looking too cold or functional, and a small table turns the kitchen into an eating area.*

design options:

left *These chunky steps have been fitted with drawers beneath the risers, with side access so that they provide useful storage for the lower level. Neat wood flooring continues up the stairs to the upper level so that the whole area looks spacious and unified.*

PLANNING PRINCIPLES

- Get to know the nature of the space you are dealing with before you think about how to decorate it – if necessary, paint it white so that you can see the shape clearly.
- Work out where the light falls, where there are dark, dull corners and which areas feel most comfortable at which times of day.
- Plan what you need the space for and how you will use it.
- Draw up an accurate floor plan to scale and clearly mark on all the unmovable features.
- Mark likely positions for essential pieces of furniture.
- Identify key areas, i.e. corners and expanses of wall, to keep clear and free from shelving and other storage items or accessories.
- **STOP** – do not do any remodelling, colour-scheming or shopping until you have checked the Design Principles in the following chapter.

Plan likely positions for these pieces, leaving plenty of room for walking around them, stretching legs, opening cupboards and drawers and so on. Next add smaller items whose positions can be more flexible and that can, if necessary, be removed from the plan if space is proving limited. If you want to try out several different layouts, cut out pieces of card to represent the furniture so that you can move them around until you are happy with the plan.

Be led by the shape of the room, the light it gets, how it fits with the rest of the space and how you are going to use it. But remember that you sometimes have to waste a bit of space in order to create the impression of it – that sense of largesse, of being able to afford to throw it away, automatically makes the place feel bigger. Leaving corners unfilled and bare areas of wall creates more of an illusion of space than cramming in as much as possible.

REASSESSING YOUR FURNITURE

Unless you are starting from scratch, you will have existing furniture – pieces you have accumulated from previous homes that will not necessarily suit the plans you have for this one. Try not to feel too attached to these. You may have a few favourite or valuable items that you definitely want to keep, but otherwise you should be as flexible as possible. This is the time to get rid of anything that has really outworn its looks or usefulness. Decide whether or not each item can be updated, painted, re-covered or recycled to match the look you have in mind, and be ruthless with anything that cannot.

finding extra space

You do not want to cram every inch of your home with shelves and cupboards, but you will probably need more storage space than you have. If you want to keep your living space clear and uncluttered, make the best possible use of wasted corners and unexplored angles.

What does your storage space need to house? At the very least, it will include clothes, shoes and a minimum of tableware and kitchen gadgets. On top of that you will have books, CDs, videos and any number of other personal possessions, some more important than others, and some needing more regular access than others. Photographs and letters are precious but you will not need to get at them too often, so they can be hidden away in 'closed' storage, while everyday tableware needs to be near at hand and easy to retrieve and replace.

WHERE TO LOOK

The first place to look is anywhere that provides a ready-made recess, as these slots can be fitted with storage without robbing the room of any useful space. Alcoves on either side of a chimney breast can be transformed into shelves, cupboards or hanging space, and are deep enough to take chunky equipment like televisions, music systems and microwaves. Shallower alcoves are perfect for books and CDs. Fireplaces themselves are useful spaces: if the fireplace is no longer functioning, or you are happy to forgo the idea of an open fire, you can remove the fittings and reline the space to provide a deep, practical recess.

It is up to you to decide whether you leave these storage spaces open or front them with cupboard doors. Doors can give the room a neater, more streamlined finish by continuing the line of the wall, but remember that you will need space for doors to open into the room. To solve this problem, either fit sliding doors, or aim for a series of narrow doors, each one exposing just a small section of storage.

above *Glass or perspex furniture minimizes the intrusive effect of larger pieces: a glass-topped table will appear to take up less space than one of solid wood. Use potentially wasted space in corners and beneath sloping ceilings to fit cupboards and store clutter out of the way.*

Remember the prioritizing process you went through earlier in the chapter – you may have to make sacrifices to create effective storage for the things that really matter to you. You will find more information on how to prune your possessions in the section on Clutter Control (see page 36).

UNLIKELY AREAS

Do not waste high-level areas that can be used for storage without getting in the way of the room. Shelves fixed at picture-rail height and above doorways will probably need a stepladder to reach them, but can be used for effective display, or for books and other items that you do not need to access very often. Usable space is often wasted behind doors, either because you do not think of looking there or because the door itself blocks off the space. There is probably enough available wall for a set of narrow bookshelves, or you could consider rehanging the door from the other side to free up extra space.

At ground level, make use of spare space under beds and other larger items of furniture. Baskets, crates, boxes and trays, perhaps on wheels, can be slotted underneath and pulled out like drawers.

An efficient way of providing extra storage is to create double-skin walls, with shelves and cupboards built into the hollow interior so that they can be accessed by doors on both sides of the wall. You can even build shallow bookshelves into the doorframe, as this will be the same thickness as the wall into which it is fitted.

However, do not feel obliged to use every available space for storage. Larger 'pockets' such as landings and the space under the stairs may be just big enough to create miniature rooms and take a desk, chair or even a small bed to accommodate overnight guests.

left *If you are happy to do without an open fire, fireplaces and chimney breasts can be hollowed out to create recesses for shelves and furniture storage. This space is the perfect size to hold a collection of folding chairs that are only needed when the table is in use: the rest of the time they are slotted neatly out of the way.*

design options:

STORAGE CHECKLIST

Check through your possessions under the following headings, and decide whether they should be out on show, easily accessible or stored away until they are needed.

- Clothes and shoes
- Coats, umbrellas and other outdoor accessories
- Linen and towels
- Books and magazines
- CDs and videos
- Kitchenware and gadgets
- China and glassware
- DIY tools and gadgets
- Files and office work
- Letters, bills and household documents
- Personal papers
- Photographs, scrapbooks, old theatre programmes and other memorabilia
- Works of art, porcelain, designer glass and other collectables

VERTICAL THINKING

Conversion flats have often been carved out of tall, high-ceilinged houses, with rooms chopped up by partition walls so that the proportions have been spoilt. Redress the balance and make use of the wasted space either by building a gallery or platform sleeping area, or by fitting high-level shelf and cupboard storage.

creating an action plan

By now, you should have a basic idea of what you want to do to each room of your home. How you proceed from here depends partly on which jobs you can tackle yourself, and partly on which rooms are most important to you.

If you are making over an entire house, the advice is often to start at the top and work down, so that you can clear up the rubble and mess as you go, but the chances are that certain rooms will take priority for personal reasons. For many people, having a comfortable, well-designed bathroom is a priority from the start, so that you have somewhere to unwind while the rest of the house is in chaos. For others, a relaxing sitting room will have the same appeal. The kitchen is important, but as long as you have a set of working appliances, the decorating can wait until later; whereas, if you work from home, a functioning office with power and telephone points is essential.

Try to resist tackling a particular feature on a whim. Work out your priorities and distinguish between what is urgent and what can wait.

WORKING ORDER

Projects can get put off indefinitely if you cannot decide where to start. The kitchen cabinets need replacing, but you really want to change the whole layout because the sink is in the wrong place, and you cannot do that until you have moved a window, and so on...

The unappealing fact is that structural work has to come first, which includes moving windows and treating any damaged timbers. The next stage is to tackle any plumbing and electrical work, so this is the time to think about

left *Furniture raised on legs, such as this low-level sideboard, gives a more spacious effect. The classic chaise-longue, with its single arm and low back, is a neater option than a conventional two- or three-seater sofa.*

design options:

WORKING CHECKLIST

- Structural work
- Plumbing and electrics
- Stripping old paintwork and wallpaper
- Replastering if necessary
- Stripping floors
- Laying new flooring
- Decorating
- Furnishing

left *White walls, stripped wood floors and recessed ceiling lighting maximize the sense of space in this room. The supporting column in the far corner creates a strong vertical line that makes the ceiling appear higher, and the two 'stepped' walls on the left add interesting perspective to the room's sightlines.*

where you want light fittings and, if you are planning to rearrange your kitchen or bathroom, decide on the layout.

You can then get on with stripping back old paintwork and wallpaper, and do any necessary replastering (you will need to allow plenty of time in your schedule for it to dry before painting or papering). If you are planning to strip floors, do it now: it creates masses of dust, so do not wait until you have painted the room. New flooring can be laid at this stage, but needs to be covered with dustsheets while you decorate.

Work out a practical timetable, thinking about which parts of the work are likely to be most disruptive (for example, when water and gas may need to be switched off). Plan around these dates, if necessary by moving out for a few days or going on holiday. You may also want to arrange for children and pets to be out of the way when you are painting, varnishing and floor-sanding.

Certain principles apply to any effective room design. Small spaces have special requirements, which mean that these principles need to be followed even more rigorously. Colour, lighting and pattern will all play their part, and it is more important than ever to choose and position your furniture astutely. The shape, style and the material it is made of will all have an effect on the final look, and you want to make sure that it flatters the space rather than disrupts it.

The good thing is that many of the space-making principles – plain surfaces, light colours, streamlined furniture shapes – overlap naturally with key modern design ingredients. Trying to create space and reduce clutter is not so easy if your taste is for flouncy curtains and four-poster beds, but with glass bricks, recessed lighting, linen blinds and sleek wooden floors, you are already halfway there.

Following these principles will help you get the best out of the existing space and may eliminate the need for walls to be pulled down or rooms knocked through. Clever colours and optical illusions can make ceilings feel higher, corridors wider and rooms larger without moving any walls. And if you discipline yourself into being more selective with your furniture and more organized about your storage, you will win back space you never realized you had.

2 DESIGN PRINCIPLES

colour

below *This cool scheme blends contemporary colours with classic design. Modern surfaces include steel and glass, and plain blinds accent the room's angles.*

Colour is the crucial factor that brings rooms of all sizes to life, making an instant impact in establishing their mood and defining their shape. The first principle to take on board is the fact that light colours make rooms look bigger.

In a small living room, whites and creams are the most obvious choices for wall colours. They are simple and elegant, providing a neutral background against which to arrange furniture, pictures and artefacts. The brightest whites establish a stark, cool environment, good for functional warehouse-style apartments and for creating a studio-like setting if you have pieces of art you want to display.

Bright white may be too cool, though, if the room does not benefit from much natural sunlight. You could be better off choosing a creamy, parchment white or one of the many alternative whites now available from paint companies. It is actually quite hard to find a pure white paint unless you opt for basic 'trade white' but there are hundreds of 'designer' whites that let you choose just the right level of cool or warmth and the exact depth of tone you want to suit the setting.

The traditional view is that keeping to one colour makes spaces look bigger by creating a single, unified effect as far as the eye can see. But rooms need accent and definition, in the same way that punctuation clarifies the meaning of a sentence. Natural shadows will provide their own subtle contrasts, and by mixing whites and creams together, you will find that you can emphasize variety of tone and give your neutral background a richer feel without actually changing the scheme and adding any definite colour. Try layering them together, for instance with cream sofas against white walls, or bright white woodwork highlighting an off-white staircase, and you will get the benefit of both warm and cool tones.

DEEPER NEUTRALS

The next level of colour up from whites and off-whites is the deeper, richer palette of stone, taupe, coffee and chocolate – elegant, contemporary shades that blend beautifully together and have a natural affinity with modern

left *Despite the room's traditional architectural style, it has a simple, understated feel that owes much to the modern lines of the boxy sofa and the little steel-legged table beside it. Layers of textured rugs and throws are used to prevent the scheme from looking cold or uninviting.*

colours

WHITES & CREAMS

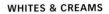

DEEPER NEUTRALS

furniture shapes and textures. You will still need to pay careful attention to the balance of warm and cool tone in the room: greys, some stone shades and even a few of the greener taupes will have a distinctly cool effect, while coffee, chocolate and the pinkier, creamier neutrals will add more warmth.

Do not try to mix too many shades together: for a practical working palette, stick to a pale shade for walls and floors (or a slighter darker one for the floor), then build up layers against this neutral background, adding items of furniture in mid tones and accessories in a mixture of mid and dark tones.

ADDING TEXTURE

Where colour is this restrained, texture becomes more important in providing contrast and character. Natural floorcoverings such as coir, sisal, seagrass and jute – all perfect for contemporary rooms – will contribute instant texture and an element of understated pattern in their weave. Mellow, natural surfaces such as leather and wood will contrast effectively with smooth polished metal and glass, and different kinds of fabric will supply a variety of interesting textures – from thick slubby linens to crisp cotton and calico, smooth velvet and suede and soft woven woollens.

STRONGER COLOUR

How much you introduce other colours depends on how important it is to you that the space looks as large as possible. The stronger the colour, the more it will seem to advance, making the walls close in and the rooms look smaller, so colour needs to be carefully handled. You may decide that some areas (bedrooms and dining rooms, for example) do not need to feel so spacious and might actually benefit from feeling warmer and more enclosed. See the chapters on individual rooms for more ideas. Warm colours (reds, yellows, oranges) will increase this effect even more, while cooler shades (blues, greens and lilacs) will help the walls to appear to recede. So, in principle, pale, cool colours are the best space-makers, and deep, warm colours the least effective. However, do not automatically exclude these stronger colours when decorating small spaces. By using flashes of colour, on single walls or in alcoves, or for individual pieces of furniture rather than as a background shade dominating the entire room, you can harness the energy and vitality they add and use them to bring a neutral room to life. Provide a glimpse of strong colour in the distance – at the end of a corridor or through a doorway into another room – and you accentuate the sense of space by leading the eye onwards and alerting it to the fact that there is more to see.

The main living areas may be most relaxing in pale neutrals, but a hint of colour visible in other rooms will open up the rest of the space to intriguing possibilities and new focal points. Cupboard doors painted in bright colours, a coloured panel hung like a modern painting on a plain white wall or a designer glass vase displayed where the light shines through it and illuminates its colour – these will all add drama and energy.

For a really dramatic effect, try using areas of fluorescent paint, which has a natural reflective quality that bounces light back into the room.

This can look particularly good in children's rooms or play areas where you want the effect to be cheerful and stimulating as well as to help create the illusion of space.

ADDING PATTERN

If single colours make spaces look bigger, it follows that anything that breaks up a run of one colour has the opposite effect.

above *Bold blocks of hot reds and striking pinks are layered against one another, on the walls and floor and in the upholstery of the furniture, creating a stimulating, vibrant effect.*

colours

left *Pale blue always opens up small spaces as it is a receding colour that appears to push surfaces further away. Here, it has been used to turn a cupboard into a study: the interior, shelves and door linings have all been painted the same colourwashed shade to help the illusion of space.*

DRAMA QUEENS

Dominant patterns are best avoided in small rooms unless you want to make a feature of the cosy, intimate feel, as they can create a frantic, over-busy impression that can be distinctly uncomfortable to live with.

If you are tired of flat painted walls, try a colourwashed effect that softens the surface with a textured look without adding any obvious sense of pattern. You could also try small,

discreet patterns, such as tiny floral sprigs, or checks or dots, which have a neat, contained look that can work well in bedrooms and children's rooms. The other type of pattern that is worth considering is a subtle stripe, which can enhance the height or width of the room if you use it judiciously. See the section on Optical Illusions, page 48, for further details on how to employ stripes effectively.

natural light

Natural light opens up a space and gives it character. It is inevitably limited by the size and direction of the windows, but you can still coax more light out of gloomy rooms by keeping the windows clear and free from clutter, and also by using reflective surfaces in order to magnify what light is already there.

The unwritten rule for contemporary window dressing is that less is more. With simple blinds, sandblasted glass and elegant shutters having replaced flouncy, frilly curtains, you can fulfil the dual function of keeping the style simple and maximizing the available light.

BLINDS AND PANELS

Roman and roller blinds will both allow you to soften the outline slightly with fabric panels, while restricting colour and pattern to a narrow strip at the top when the blinds are pulled up. Make them from translucent white muslin or stretched voile, and you can leave them down so that they provide privacy yet filter plenty of light into the room (perfect for bright, sunny windows). Slatted Venetian-style blinds, available in plastic, steel or wood, can switch from light-admitting to light-obscuring with just a change in their angle and suit the functional, industrial style of some modern furnishings.

Neat fabric panels, creating a cross between curtain and blind, are even simpler. Stretched on to hinged metal portière rods, they can swing open and shut like shutters. Made from sheer voile and slotted on to a fixed pole or wire across the top of the window, they act as a contemporary (and much more attractive) version of the old-fashioned net curtain, screening the window without obscuring the light.

CURTAIN OPTIONS

Do not feel that you have to eschew curtains altogether – just avoid using too much bulky fabric and too many overblown gathers which take up valuable space. Opt for long-line curtains in heavy linen or cord which contribute a sense of height and elegance, or sheer voiles, muslins or organzas which screen the glass with a filmy layer for a touch of modern romance. Keep headings simple by using tab-tops (made from fabric or leather), metal eyelet holes or clip-on rings that will slide on to a slim pole.

below *Louvred shutters outline the elegant architecture of these tall windows and filter the light to prevent this white-painted room from feeling too bright and glaring in strong summer sunlight.*

CLASSIC SHUTTERS

If the window has original shutters, make the most of them. This is a classic style that has perfect contemporary relevance. By providing architectural definition without adding decoration, shutters prove that the most elegant windows do not actually need dressing at all. If you want to add new shutters, wooden replicas of traditional shutters can be made to fit your window, or you could opt for a sleeker alternative such as plain lengths of MDF (medium-density fibreboard) hinged together, or go ultra-modern with panels of white perspex.

above *A simple curtain, which has been folded at the top to form a deep pelmet, is all this small window needs to shade it. A neat ribbon trim along the lower edge provides a touch of colour to match the woodwork of the window and deep sill.*

above right *Classic folding shutters are perfect for kitchens as they keep the space free of unnecessary fabrics. The shutters have been painted in a shade that coordinates with the wall tiles, and the deep window sills create extra work surfaces.*

ETCHED OR FROSTED GLASS

A subtle option, if you are sure the window does not need a clear view, is to let the glass provide its own screen. Glass can be sandblasted by specialist glaziers (at a cost) to create an etched or frosted effect, incorporating individual designs such as street numbers or abstract patterns. Or you can create your own look by spraying on instant frosting (available from art and craft shops or suppliers) or by applying adhesive film designs.

reflected light

Another way in which you can boost the level of natural light is by adding surfaces that bounce it back into the room.

USING MIRRORS

Mirrors are the most obvious source: a huge mirror on one wall of a small room will double the perceived space, both by increasing the available light and by showing a reflected image, making it appear twice the size. Position it where it reflects a view that makes an impact as you enter the room. Avoid hanging it opposite another mirror, or you will just get a series of ever-decreasing identical images. A panel of mirrored glass fitted into an alcove will achieve the same effect more subtly, as without the edges of the mirror being visible, the illusion that the reflection is part of the room itself is more convincing. A collection of smaller mirrors grouped like a picture display will achieve a similar effect.

OTHER REFLECTIVE SURFACES

Chrome-framed furniture, aluminium flooring and worktops, brushed steel kitchen appliances – all these surfaces have a reflective quality that will help make the space look lighter and bigger.

left *Reflective steel surfaces bounce light back into this kitchen, making the most of the spots recessed into the base of the wall units, and keeping the whole effect sleek and cool. Shiny worktops, drawer fronts, splashbacks and appliances all contribute to the finish and create a single unified surface.*

design options:

SURFACES THAT REFLECT LIGHT

- Mirror
- Metal
- Glass
- Polished wood
- Polished leather
- High-gloss paint and lacquered finishes
- Satin fabrics
- Glazed ceramics (tiles and china)

left *A wall composed of glass bricks will let light through from one room to another while still maintaining privacy – the perfect compromise between solid walls and open-plan living. Chrome fittings and accessories will add extra reflection.*

And smaller accessories with a lustred or polished finish will catch the light and harness its space-making potential. To this end, choose ceramic tiles for kitchens and bathrooms, opt for glazed ceramics and glassware in dining rooms and introduce satin bedspreads and crystal chandeliers in a romantic bedroom.

Similarly, instead of adding displays of cut flowers, which can appear fussy as well as being light-absorbent, try filling a plain glass container – the plainer the better, so look for simple tanks rather than fancy vases – with marbles or glass nuggets, to provide more contemporary, light-reflective decoration.

left *This wall-mounted uplighter casts a beam that washes the wall with a soft glow and screens the light source from view. The matt steel light fitting adds a functional, understated feel to the corner.*

31

planning your lighting

below *Clustered steel pendant lights on long flexes create a dramatic effect that makes the bright metal part of the design scheme. The bulbs are hidden and the beams are directed downwards, while the flexes echo the upright steel bars of the gallery.*

Lighting needs to fulfil three key functions. Firstly, it needs to provide enough background light for general use, in effect recreating natural daylight. This is known as ambient lighting. Secondly, it needs to supply focused light for specific areas such as desks, bathroom mirrors and kitchen worktops. This is known as task lighting. Lastly, it needs to create areas of interest and variety, highlighting or softening the architecture of the room and adding atmosphere with shadows and contrasts – this is accent lighting. Different rooms will need you to shift the emphasis from one type to another. For example, studies need good task lighting whereas accent lighting is key to designing a restful bedroom. Usually a combination of all three will establish the right levels of mood and practicality.

MODERN APPROACHES

There was a time when the three types of light were clearly defined by their fittings and positions. Ambient light was provided by a central pendant fitting, task light by reading lamps on desks and fluorescent strips beneath kitchen wall cabinets and accent light by a scattering of table lamps. Today, things are more subtle and sophisticated and it is often hard to tell which light is performing which function.

This is partly because lighting has been recognized as a point of interest in its own right. There is more appreciation of its function and a utilitarian approach with no frills or coyness, so that light bulbs no longer need to be disguised. Spotlights are clamped baldly on to tracks and stands and strip lights come in bright colours to create dramatic glowing features like something from the Starship Enterprise. Now you can even buy plug-in glass blocks that look like a standard light bulb frozen in a giant ice-cube, making a design feature of the part we always tried so hard to hide under tasteful shades.

The other difference with modern lighting is that more planning goes into positioning and directing the beam, so that it 'washes' the edges of the space and defines it without emphasizing the boundaries or highlighting any imperfections in the surface of the wall. In small rooms, for instance, lighting acquires extra importance because the human eye reads distances instinctively and uses light to gauge dimensions. Fit lights in the furthest points of the room and you highlight those distances and expand the space.

design options:

Also look for places where the beam will highlight interesting angles and cast intriguing shadows: position lights behind beams or pillars, or in alcoves or so that the glow appears from behind a 'floating' ceiling or wall.

A LIGHTING PLAN

If possible, you need to design your lighting plan before you decorate so that you can put wiring in place, fixing wall lights and recessing spotlights into the ceiling before you paint the surfaces. But all is not lost if you have not managed to do this. Track-mounted spots can be wired into a standard ceiling fitting, and as long as you have plenty of power points (aim for at least two in each corner of an average-sized room), you will find the best plug-in designs are portable enough to make an impact wherever you put them. Adjustable or jointed desk lamps with metal shades feel more up-to-date than fabric designs.

CEILING LIGHTS

There is still a place for ceiling-hung lights if the fittings are right. Shades in understated paper, glass, acrylic or perspex will be suitably contemporary, and droplet-hung chandeliers create their own sense of style. The concept may be traditional, but as long as the furnishings are simply tailored or casual and Bohemian, rather than chintzy and formal, their sparkling, multi-reflective light can look ultra-cool.

BULB TYPES

Different bulbs will provide a different quality of light, so choose them according to the atmosphere you want to create.

- **Tungsten filament** The traditional all-purpose bulb, which comes in a variety of shapes and wattage – the higher the wattage, the brighter and whiter the light.
- **Internally silvered reflector** Half-silvered with a reflective coating to bounce the light downwards, suitable for spotlights.

- **Tungsten halogen** A tungsten filament that interacts with halogen gas, giving a brighter, whiter light, good for creating designer effects. Free-standing halogen lamps cannot be plugged into a normal domestic socket without the use of a transformer.

below This sleek scheme combines tiny, discreet recessed spotlights with neat adjustable lamps that can be redirected wherever you want the beams to fall.

LIGHTING SOLUTIONS

- For instant designer light, try halogen bulbs fitted into transformer boxes that can be plugged into power points wherever you want them. The beam can range from a narrow 8-degree focus to a much wider 50-degree flood. This varies the effect, so try them in different positions – floors, shelves and tabletops. Use the slightly more expensive faceted (dichroic) bulbs for extra sparkle.
- If you want to wire in new lighting, bear in mind that it is easier to fit uplighters in floors than to fix wall lights or ceiling-recessed downlighters, because taking up a couple of floorboards is less disruptive than cutting into finished walls and ceilings.
- Dimmer switches are an excellent addition, giving you instant control over light levels and the opportunity to adjust the mood of the room for different occasions and at various times of the day.

BASEMENT FLATS

It is particularly important to get the lighting right in basement flats where lack of daylight can create big problems. Clever lighting can effectively disguise the underground setting, dispelling gloom and creating wonderful effects (although to enjoy the full benefits, you will probably need to keep it switched on all day). As ceilings will invariably be lower here, avoid ceiling-hung lights and concentrate on wall and floor fittings and free-standing lamps.

furniture

Furniture should never be chosen in isolation from the surroundings it is going to occupy, and this is especially important where space is in limited supply. However accurately you think you can envisage what it will look like, dimensions are always deceptive.

Never go shopping for furniture without a full set of measurements recording the available space and a tape-measure to check the size of any piece you are planning to buy – not just so that you can be sure it will fit into the space, but also to check that it suits the proportions of the room. Small rooms need smaller-scale furniture to keep the whole effect balanced, so be particularly careful with large pieces like sofas and dining tables. Scaled-down furniture will make the room look bigger. In the UK, the Georgians used this principle to great effect, and it still holds good for small modern homes.

Think about shape, too, and look for neat, compact designs such as square-cut boxy shapes that follow the angles of the room. Streamlined curves also work well, as they take up less room than outward-splaying scroll arms or old-fashioned wing chairs. Tapering designs, such as upright chairs with backs that narrow towards the top, will also create an illusion of more space.

Avoid unnecessary details such as pelmets and ruffles that spoil the clean lines and, again, aim for plain colours rather than patterned fabrics so that the furniture does not break up the room too much. Try to maintain a sense of space and light around individual pieces: sofas and armchairs that are raised slightly on legs will often look less obtrusive than designs that sit solidly on the floor. Make use of transparent materials that blend into the background: glass-topped tables and moulded perspex chairs have a barely-there quality which is brilliant for restricted dining areas, for example.

ADDITIONAL FEATURES

If space is really tight, look for folding and stacking designs, and furniture on wheels that can be pushed out of the way when not in use. Chunky castors can be bought individually for fixing on to furniture legs and adding instant mobility. And you will find all sorts of dual-purpose designs that double your space by providing two pieces of furniture in one. Blanket boxes supply storage inside and a coffee table on top. Ottomans fulfil a similar role but with a

design options:

padded top creating extra seating. Choose the right linen basket and it will do double duty as a seat in the bathroom, where space is always limited. Look for ladder radiators here, too, which provide towel rails as well as heating.

LAYOUT AND POSITION

Let the shape of the room dictate the layout of the furniture, placing pieces where they flatter its proportions. Do not see it as a challenge to fit as much into the space as possible. This is the time to be ruthless with your possessions: discard any furniture that does not benefit the layout and that is not strictly necessary for practical comfort. Do not feel obliged to keep sets of furniture complete. If there is only room for one armchair in the sitting room, consign its partner to the bedroom or study. If the dining table looks better with four chairs rather than six, redistribute the remaining two among other rooms until they are needed. A well-designed room looks right from the moment you enter it,

with focal points and sightlines providing good views across it, and enough space to get where you want without falling over unnecessary furniture. Remember that empty space is just as important to the shape of the room. The less furniture you can get away with, the more spacious the room will feel.

THEORY INTO PRACTICE

These principles are intended to guide you, not restrict you, so do not get too bogged down by the theory. Try things out for yourself, follow your gut feelings and be led by the individual qualities and requirements of your particular space. There are times when you need to be cautious about making expensive and irreversible changes – such as demolishing walls – but you can go on rearranging the furniture endlessly until you are happy with the effect.

below *Seating units that can be pushed together in different configurations or used separately are useful where space is short.*

FITTED FURNITURE

● Bear in mind that fitted furniture generally makes more effective use of space than free-standing pieces, creating a sleek finish and providing far more storage. Shallow shelves or cupboards fitted floor-to-ceiling along one wall of a room will offer ample storage for books, CDs, tableware and other essentials while being less obtrusive than a selection of individual cabinets and bookcases.

clutter control

below *Deep storage drawers have been fitted under this bed to keep clutter out of the way without the need for incorporating extra furniture that would reduce the available floor space in the room.*

Small spaces and clutter just do not mix. If you have too much stuff, it will spoil the look of a room, confuse the eye and generally get in the way. Also take into consideration that clutter influences how you feel: it is far easier to be relaxed and comfortable if your surroundings are calm and organized.

Our homes are under constant attack from clutter. There is the stuff that accumulates daily almost like dust (newspapers, magazines, bills, laundry) and there are things that you acquire gradually over the years (books, clothes, photographs, furniture). The first group simply needs to be dealt with regularly to keep it under control. The second is more of a problem because it invades the house slowly and imperceptibly, so that you do not realize how much of it you have until your space actually becomes less usable because of it. There are three key elements to effective clutter control: you need to be selective about your possessions, you need to display or store them astutely and you also need to discipline yourself into clear-thinking, anti-clutter habits.

THROWING OUT FURNITURE
Furniture is particularly difficult to say goodbye to because there is an inevitable sense that it is useful. But getting rid of it will become easier as you clear out other clutter. Extra cupboards and chests of drawers will simply become redundant if you let go of unworn clothes and footwear, unused gadgets and packs of unnecessary photographs.

design options:

BEING SELECTIVE

The secret is to take control of your surroundings and choose your possessions – do not let them choose you. That means throwing out anything you have not used or worn in the last 12 months. If it has been waiting to be cleaned or mended, then make a decision: either get it done, have it recycled into something useful or get rid of it.

Eliminate duplicate items, too. You will probably have a favourite you use out of choice, whether it is a stepladder, hair dryer or kitchen measuring jug, so ditch the seconds instead of hoarding them for reserve use. The same goes for books and CDs: weed out spare copies and take the rest to a charity shop.

Do not hoard packs of old photographs that you are never going to look at. Select the ones you want to keep and put them into albums or frames. Be ruthless about throwing away the ones you do not really like or want. You can always keep the negatives and have reprints made if you suffer nostalgia pangs later.

Work through all your possessions like this, deciding whether you really want things or if they have just attached themselves to you. Tackle one area at a time so that it does not feel too brutal: clothes one week, kitchen gadgets another, books and CDs the next, and so on.

ORGANIZED STORAGE

What you do decide to keep needs to be stored safely, where you can find it again. Do not just throw things in a cupboard and shut the door on them: if you are prepared to abandon them

left *Colourful crates lined up on deep shelves are labelled with their contents to provide an organized storage system for games, files, clothes and so on. A system like this can be used to colour-code your possessions to make access easier.*

CLUTTER-CLEARING BASICS

- Throw out anything unused for 12 months or more, or recycle it into something that you will use.
- Get rid of any items of furniture that are taking up significant space without adding to the look or practicality of the room.
- Invest in boxes and baskets to store newspapers, bills, appliance controls and anything else you usually leave lying around.
- Reclaim your surfaces. You do not have to use every shelf and tabletop for storage or display – leave some of them empty and spacious.
- Put things away as soon as you have finished with them: books back on shelves, tools in their box, clothes in cupboards or laundry baskets.
- Buy purpose-built cupboards and units fitted with compartments for organized storage – you are more likely to be encouraged to put things away if you know exactly where you can find them again.
- Look for furniture with hidden storage assets – beds fitted with drawers, dining tables with chair slots in the base, coffee tables with lift-up lids.
- Fit doors across any alcoves and spaces under stairs: they are bound to end up as unofficial dumping grounds, so screen them off in anticipation of their use for storage.
- Avoid glass-fronted cabinets if you cannot keep their contents tidy: you are better off hiding things from view behind solid doors.

to this fate, you might as well have thrown them away completely. If they are not needed immediately, create filing systems for them with boxes, bags and crates, and label things clearly so that you know what is what. Avoid cardboard boxes, which are susceptible to damp and rot. Wrap fragile items in bubblewrap – again, if you cannot be bothered, you probably do not care enough about the item to keep it.

Create organized storage wherever possible, using cube systems and stacking units, and look for furniture that provides hidden storage space in tables and stools and under beds. Best of all, build shallow floor-to-ceiling shelves and

cupboards along an entire wall to provide masses of slimline storage while shaving only a fraction off the room's floor area.

NEAT THINKING

Keep the hallway clear to start off on the right footing, and the rest of the house will follow in the same vein. Store coats, keys and mail neatly. Deal with bills, letters and other paperwork as it arrives, and then file it away. And do not let messages, addresses and phone numbers loiter on untidy scraps of paper – transfer the information to your diary or address book and throw away the notes.

STORING BOOKS

To some people, books help furnish a room; to others, they are simply unnecessary clutter. If you want them on show, make sure you have enough shelves to keep them neatly displayed (see left). Otherwise, create ample slimline closed-door storage to keep them out of sight.

left *The simple fireplace maintains the room's contemporary feel, with a plain lintel acting as a mantelpiece and the recess painted to match the rest of the room.*

opposite above *Clever cupboards have been built into this white-painted column, so that they are completely hidden when they are closed but still provide useful storage for anything from glassware to videos and DVDs.*

opposite *Chunky shelves fixed at different heights create practical storage for various sizes of books and files. A classic leather suitcase provides extra space for videos, while giving a less hi-tech appearance.*

Do not hang on to old newspapers and magazines: clear your newspapers at the end of each day. Cut out any features you want to keep and file them, then put out the remains for rubbish or recycling. Be selective about which magazines you keep. If you subscribe to a favourite publication, start a separate shelf to house your collection. Otherwise, keep a few current issues for the bathroom (they are probably more use there than cluttering up precious surfaces in the living room), and ditch the rest once you have read them.

If you know you have not got the time to deal with everything on a daily basis, invest in boxes and baskets to hold papers, bills and anything else left lying around – from books to remote controls. Do a regular collection around each room and sort them out as soon as the container is full. Then have a throw-away day once a month to get rid of anything you do not need to keep.

design principles: modern classic style

below *White walls, pale woods and elegant furniture shapes create a restrained background for the modern classic look – airy, light-filled, very spacious and effortlessly relaxing.*

This is the look that you instantly associate with 'modern' – cool, restrained, neutral and tasteful. It says loft apartment, warehouse conversion, contemporary art gallery – smart, minimal and sophisticated. It also says 'space', because of its clean lines and pale colours.

Like all apparently effortless achievements, the simple, straightforward appearance of the modern classic style requires rigorous discipline and is more complex than it might seem, involving a careful balancing of contrasts and paradoxes. The general effect, for instance, is elegant and easy on the eye because of the understated colours and lack of frantic pattern. However, this can also make the room look over-edgy and industrial rather than comfortable enough to spend time in.

The direction it takes depends ultimately on the materials you use and the sharpness of furniture and architectural angles. For maximum edge, include plenty of glass and metal, and go for square-cut, boxy furniture shapes. To boost the comfort factor, look for streamlined curves, which will feel more luxurious and soften the hard edges by shifting the balance from sleek, reflective surfaces to absorbent, textural materials. One of the greatest subtleties of modern classic style is the way it combines restraint and comfort. Understated, 'masculine' fabrics such as wool, tweed, corduroy and leather in neutral colours provide a neat, tailored effect and a really good sense of line, and yet at the same time are wonderfully warm, tactile and sensual.

TIMELESS MINIMALISM

It is also a look that adapts seamlessly from day to night-time use. The pale, reflective colours and polished surfaces will flood the room with light and create the perfect functional working space during the day, and then appear elegant, minimal and very sophisticated at night, especially if softened by additional textures like velvety suede and corduroy. There is also an affinity with Japanese minimalism, because of the restrained lines and neutral colours: to emphasize this particular oriental look, include contrasting surfaces such as textured paper and bamboo set against sleek polished lacquer.

below *White walls, pale woods and elegant furniture shapes create a restrained background for the modern classic look – airy, light-filled, very spacious and effortlessly relaxing.*

left *Leather is one of the materials that translates perfectly from age to age. Smart and functional in elegant shapes, it adds a sense of timeless style to modern settings and furnishings.*

MAINTAINING THE LOOK

Just remember that, for modern classic style, less is more. The finished result may look eminently practical with its clean lines, unfussy design and plain wooden floors, but this is a grown-up look that demands to be taken seriously and takes a lot of maintenance. Clutter control is essential, and all your furnishing choices need careful editing: if you cannot decide whether to include something or not, leave it out.

Where to use this look

Virtually anywhere – its ultimate success factor is that it is so classic, you really cannot go wrong.

WARMING IT UP

Do not let the overall effect become too cool, clinical and remote, or acquire the characterless perfection of a showhouse – it needs to feel lived in as well as looking good. To warm it up and relax it a little without fear of ruining the style,

try incorporating a few simple, robust fabrics such as denim, calico and striped mattress ticking, all of which have a natural, workaday quality which is in keeping with the clean lines but also feels slightly more casual.

design options:

FURNISHING INGREDIENTS

Select ingredients from the following list to put together your own take on modern classic style.

colours and textures
- White or off-white walls
- Deeper neutrals (grey, coffee, chocolate) for fabrics, flooring and upholstery
- Plain wood floors (parquet or boards)
- Minimal pattern
- Clean lines

furniture
- Pale wood furniture and kitchen cabinets
- Frosted glass kitchen cabinet fronts
- Square-cut, boxy furniture (including corner sofas)
- Brushed steel and aluminium kitchen appliances
- Glass and perspex furniture and doors
- Low-level furniture

fabrics
- Leather
- Suede
- Corduroy
- Sheepskin
- Cotton
- Tweed
- Flannel
- Striped mattress ticking
- Linen
- Denim
- Calico

design principles: modern romantic style

'Romantic' tends to have a ring of old-fashioned formality about it, but the latest looks give romance a modern twist, adding unstructured, slightly Bohemian elements to create a style that is relaxed and casual – nothing too fancy or frilly.

Despite its floaty fabrics and slightly more cluttered character, the modern romantic look is excellent for decorating small spaces because the colours are pale, the surfaces sparkling and light-reflective and the overall feel gentle and easy to live with.

The key to modern romance is a delicate touch that makes everything look doubly elegant. Ironically, this may involve introducing furniture and accessories more usually associated with earlier periods, simply because older designs tend to be smaller. Graceful furniture such as sweeping sleighbeds and the pretty carved Scandinavian designs of the 18th-century Gustavian period are painted in white or soft pastel shades to highlight their shape. The pieces themselves tend to be small and slim: narrow console tables that will stand flat against a hall wall, little writing desks that are just the right size to fit beneath a window and tall-legged side tables that take up a minimal amount of space beside a bed or sofa.

Antique sofas and chairs, the sort with a carved wooden or gilded frame, are usually more compact and less solid in appearance than their modern counterparts. Intricate wrought iron – for bedsteads, sofas and little bedroom chairs – has the same lightweight effect. Here, the open-worked design provides a sort of filigree pattern that seems to take up less space than solid materials, in the same way that the tracery of lace appears transparent in comparison with tightly woven fabrics.

ROMANTIC FABRICS

Romantic fabrics add extra delicacy, and tend to be virtually translucent, or light-reflective or both – the perfect combination where space is short.

above *The decorative wrought-iron bed frame, ornamental chandelier and iridescent satin bed covers add a flourish of romance to an otherwise simple setting. The shuttered window and chunky wall shelves reinforce the plain lines of the room.*

KEEP IT SIMPLE
Do not let the feminine touch lapse into the frilly, fussy and old-fashioned. Keep the overall look simple with painted floorboards instead of carpets and painted furniture instead of polished wood.

top *Pinks and lilacs combine to create a pretty, light-reflective background for simple styles and modern paintings. Painting the folding doors soft blue transforms them from practical to intriguing and surprising – more like a Japanese screen.*

above *Crystal droplets and fine decorative metalwork are part of the Bohemian tradition that characterizes modern romantic style. Delicate and graceful, they provide striking contrasts with plain colours and modern furniture styles.*

Lace curtains may be too old-fashioned for modern settings, but the contemporary alternatives – full-length panels of sheer voile and muslin – provide just enough privacy without blocking the light. And because they are so thin and flimsy, you can combine several layers together to increase the sense of romantic decadence without cluttering up the room with too much bulky fabric. Look for shimmering pearlescent fabrics, too: pretty starched organza (the kind little girls' party dresses used to be made of) makes elegant cushion covers, and satins and silks can be layered together as throws on beds and sofas for the ultimate in modern luxury.

MODERN TRADITIONAL

Modern romantic style is full of elements that verge on the traditional but are used in a contemporary way (that is why you have to be careful to avoid lapsing into the frilly pitfalls). So, for instance, the classic crystal waterfall chandelier has been replaced by simpler designs that are less formal than their country-house ancestors. This means you can use them in settings like kitchens and bathrooms as well as the more usual sitting rooms and bedrooms.

This sense of the unexpected is another hallmark of romantic style: it is about breaking the rules and sprinkling a dash of glamour in rooms where practicality is usually the yardstick. For instance, flamboyant Venetian-style engraved mirrors will transform functional bathrooms into luxurious retreats, coloured glass doorknobs and curtain pole finials add sparkle to the most basic of accessories and crystal droplets can be stitched along curtain tops, around lampshades and even on to curtain fabric to catch the light with their faceted surfaces.

Where to use this look

Sitting rooms and bedrooms; halls, bathrooms and functional spaces that need glamorizing.

design options:

FURNISHING INGREDIENTS
Select ingredients from the following list to put together your own take on modern romantic style.

colours and textures
- Whites and creams
- Pale grey
- Pastels (especially mauves and blues)
- Mother-of-pearl
- Lustred ceramics
- Crystal and glass

furniture
- Elegant painted furniture
- Painted wrought iron (white, pastel or gilded)
- Little antique chairs and sofas
- Roll-top baths
- French-style daybeds
- Sleighbeds

fabrics
- Satins
- Embroidered silks
- Floral prints
- Organza
- Muslin
- Lace
- Voile
- Pearlescent fabrics

decorative details
- Crystal light fittings and droplet decorations
- Crystal doorknobs and curtain pole finials
- Simple floaty window dressings
- White or cream painted floorboards
- Gold and silver leaf decoration
- Venetian engraved mirrors

design principles: modern utility style

The overwhelming impression of the modern utility look is one of neatness, which makes it perfect for small spaces. Small-print patterns and small-scale furniture give it a doll's-house quality, reminiscent of the old adage – there is a place for everything and everything in its place.

This is a practical, organized look, with 'thrift' as its watchword, resulting in space-saving furniture, clever storage ideas and, where possible, items recycled to squeeze the last ounce of use out of them. If you are alarmed by the ultra-sleek modernity of so much contemporary style, this is a good way to introduce a few second-hand pieces, creating a softer look that has retro charm without being overtly 'antique'.

Utility style dates from a time when everything was rationed, not just space. Post-war utility furniture from the 1940s and 1950s in the UK was designed so that it used up the smallest amount of wood and involved the minimum amount of time and effort to make: hence its small-scale, unfussy shape. Everything had a function and nothing was designed purely to

right *The bright colours and small-scale patterns of the utility era of the 1940s and 1950s are easy to adapt for small modern homes. Details appropriate for this cheerful and practical look include plasticized fabrics (such as the spotted chair covers) and neat, painted woodwork.*

look good – and it is this that rescues the style from acquiring too much of a country-cottage prettiness. There is a robust, urban feel about it that makes it eminently practical and ideally suited to modern life.

Use retro styling as an excuse for budgeting, and it is the perfect reason to get away with minimal quantities of fabric – try kitchen windows screened by a simple pelmet across the top, like a post-war pantry, instead of full-blown curtains. Painted floors are also appropriate as they are much more practical than carpet, and offer a chance to change the colour scheme with very little upheaval. Restrained light fittings are key, too – think plain aluminium shades that shield you from the light rather than dispersing it.

ADDING DETAILS

The practical, workaday feel inspires a host of ideas for kitchen linens that are pretty as well as practical. Where modern classic style involves holding back and letting a few neutral, well-chosen pieces make their statement, modern utility relies on dainty patterns and cheerful

MAKING IT WORK

Don't let the effect lapse into chintzy or country house. Keep the florals in order with plenty of hard surfaces and practical features. Save the space for where it's really useful – as long as you don't clutter up a small kitchen with unnecessary furniture, you'll have room for a classic butler's sink which will suit the practical quality of utility style and provide essential food preparation space.

colours to offset the basic, functional nature of the furnishings. Which is why you can find aprons, peg bags and ironing-board covers in sprigged floral cotton fabrics which will brighten up a working kitchen.

A neat-printed wallpaper can be used to line an alcove or shelf back: the pattern would be too much if used throughout the room, but in a confined area like this it is just enough to add interest and character. Simple gathered curtains can be used to replace cabinet doors in a small kitchen. Again, used across a larger area this might appear fussy and frilly, but in a small room it merely becomes a practical solution to the problem of restricted space for opening doors.

STYLE AS A WAY OF LIFE

The entire look promotes 'neatness' as a way of thinking, with the emphasis on tidiness rather than chic. A stack of perfectly folded linen stored in a cupboard or set of open shelves or a row of wall pegs holding utensils or drawstring bags will create the effect instantly. Much of it is to do with schoolroom simplicity: wooden bench seating to help you fit more people round the dining table and old school chairs (easy to brighten up with a coat of eggshell paint) lined up against a wall to give a sense of no-nonsense practicality.

There is a touch of Shaker-style puritanism, too: the chairs could just as easily be folded and hung on the wall or slotted into a convenient alcove – it is all a question of function triumphing over style. Remember that the simplest patterns can also be practical space-making solutions: candy-striped wallpaper will make a low ceiling look higher and white tongue-and-groove panelling – the perfect background for brightly painted junk-shop chairs – will create neat vertical lines for the same effect.

Where to use this look

Use it in kitchens, bathrooms, sitting rooms, hallways and landings.

design options:

FURNISHING INGREDIENTS

Select ingredients from the following list to put together your own take on modern utility style.

colours and textures

- Painted wood (including floors and skirting boards)
- 1950s pastel colours (think American diner)
- Coloured chrome and enamel

furniture

- Utility furniture
- Second-hand chairs (especially from schools and chapels)
- Hanging racks and wall cabinets
- Chicken-wire cupboard fronts
- Roll-top baths

fabrics

- Small-scale patterns
- Sprigged florals
- Plastic and acrylic
- Crisp cottons
- Candy stripes and gingham checks

decorative details

- Wirework holders
- Laundry bags for storage
- Peg rails and coat hooks
- Tinware
- Wall-mounted plate racks
- Coloured appliances
- Second-hand mirrors in need of resilvering

design principles: modern drama style

below *Dramatic colours will help bring spaces to life by creating focal points. Here, deep shades, bold contrasts and strong shapes are combined together in clean blocks of unexpected colour.*

Flamboyant, colourful and larger than life, this is the look to go for if you want to make an instant impact. With none of the discretion and restraint of the three previous looks, this one comes out fighting and demands to be noticed.

Modern drama is not for the faint-hearted. But if you have got the courage, it will repay you amply by creating a bold, confident impression. It is a brilliant way to establish a note of distinctive individuality, partly because it overturns the usual colour convention about not using strong shades in small spaces. Used in a hallway, for instance, it will instantly intrigue visitors and alert them to the possibility of interesting rooms beyond.

But even if you do not feel entirely comfortable about employing bold colours in constantly used areas such as halls and living rooms, you can indulge your more adventurous ideas in bedrooms and bathrooms – places that will not be on public show 24 hours a day and where you can therefore afford to decorate with a little less caution.

What you are doing, in furnishing a small space in dramatic style, is refusing to give in to the limitations of the space. Instead of trying to blur the dimensions or open them up with unified stretches of pale colours and small-scale patterns, this technique involves making a positive feature of the small space. It uses bold 'advancing' colours to draw attention to walls and bring them closer. It sets contrasting shades against one another to highlight individual surfaces and break up the space. And it experiments with larger shapes and furniture designs to push the boundaries to their limits.

HIGH DRAMA

Think of it like a stage set, where the idea is to catch the audience's eye and create an illusion.

KEEP IT TASTEFUL

Do not let the patterns and colours get too frantic and out of control. Think art as well as over-the-top. If necessary, take a hint from the modern classic style (see page 40) to calm things down a little.

left A flamboyant colour scheme of reds and golds adds instant drama and turns the far room into a focal point. Although the foreground landing is narrow, you get the sense that there is more to see in the distance, which opens up the space beyond like a stage set.

design options:

FURNISHING INGREDIENTS

Select ingredients from the following list to put together your own take on modern drama style.

colours and textures
- Bold painted walls
- Strong accent colours used for individual walls and alcoves
- Contrasting colours (try blue with orange, yellow with purple)
- Psychedelic retro patterns
- Gold and silver leaf decoration

fabrics
- Bright satins and silks
- Sensuous, luxurious fabrics
- Velvet and corduroy
- Fake fur and animal prints

decorative details
- Coloured tiles
- Coloured lighting
- Huge modern paintings and prints
- Mirrored walls and cupboards
- Gilded furniture and frames
- Ornate Baroque mirrors

If you decorate as though you had more space to play with, the chances are that people will believe you. Install a luxurious roll-top bath, or create a Roman-style stepped surround by building a platform around the bath so that you can step down into it. The opulent impression will give the effect of a larger room. Hang a huge Baroque-style gilt-framed mirror and – as well as doubling the size of the room by increasing the light and reflecting the facing wall – you conjure up an expansive, extravagant look that instantly assumes more space than is actually available.

Lighting can be as helpful as mirrors in working this magic. Again, think of the stage set and remember how clever lighting is used to alter the layout and create mood and drama. Bright walls will look even more effective if light is glancing off them to create areas of glowing colour and darker tones.

COLOUR AND TEXTURE

Capitalize on the colour aspect, too, by using the walls to display contemporary pictures and prints. Bold shapes and strong colours are the things to go for – think Mark Rothko and Howard Hodgkin. For the simplest effect of all, all you need is panels of colour: paint pieces of hardboard, or stretch a length of bright fabric over it and hang it on the wall as instant art. And do not forget texture. There is something very sensuous about the dramatic look, so add furnishings with plenty of contrasting texture: soft-finished corduroy, suede and velvet alongside sleek polished leather, metal and glass.

where to use the look

Bedrooms, hallways, rooms planned for evening use; any areas in which you want to create an immediate, full-blown impact.

optical illusions

There are a whole host of simply executed visual tricks that can be used to change the feel of the space. Try some of these inventive illusions to alter the perceived shape and expand the apparent size of your rooms.

USING COLOUR

Some visual alterations can be achieved without the need for major structural work. Combine light colours (to open up the space) with other basic design principles, and you can make narrow rooms feel wider and low-ceilinged rooms much less oppressive.

For instance, taking the ceiling colour a little way down the walls – to around picture-rail height – will have the effect of making the ceiling look bigger and therefore of 'pushing' the walls apart, so that the room feels more spacious. Stairways, halls and long, corridor-like rooms will look much wider if you paint the side walls in a light colour, keeping the floor and ceiling pale, too, and making use of horizontal lines to 'push' the side walls further apart.

USING LINES

You may not want to go as far as adding definite pattern by painting stripes or hanging striped wallpaper, but you can achieve the same expanding effect by using furniture and fittings to provide their own lines.

Floorboards laid across a hallway, rather than along it, will do the trick effectively. If your stairs are carpeted, fitting the carpet to the full width of the treads rather than laying it as a central strip will make them look wider. In a narrow room, paint subtle stripes across the shorter walls to make them appear wider. Likewise, running long shelves across one of them, or standing a long table in front of it, will also help to stretch the walls visually by adding strong horizontal lines. Vertical stripes can have a similar effect on the height of the room, making it look taller and 'raising' a low ceiling.

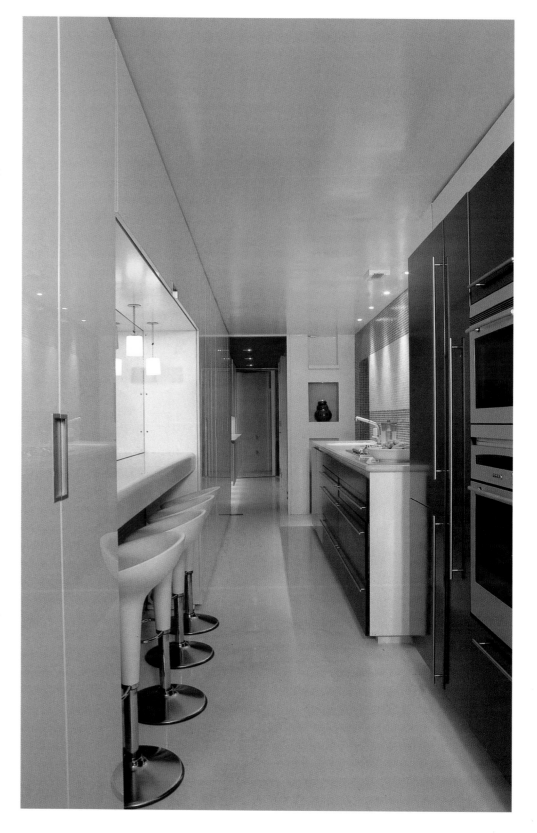

design options:

USING PERSPECTIVE

One of the most effective ways of creating more visual space is to play with the perspective of the walls. When you look at any room, the walls appear to draw slightly closer together as they recede into the distance. So if you can deliberately 'taper' the floor area of the room, this effect will be increased and the room will look longer than it actually is. You do not need to undertake any rebuilding: instead, fit full-height storage along the two longer sides, hiding useful shelves and cupboards behind doors and panels that in effect become new 'walls'. Keep the storage very shallow at the end closest to you,

gradually increasing its depth towards the far end so that you shave two wedges of space off the room and, by narrowing the room towards the far end, make it seem even further away.

CREATING DIVISIONS

Other non-structural changes can be used to redistribute the space and create different rooms or areas on a temporary basis. Make use of folding screens to turn one end of a room into a study or sleeping space, or erect your own 'wall' by positioning storage units so that they demarcate separate territory. It does not need to be a solid partition: open cube shelving can create a visual divide that stops well short of ceiling height and still admits light and a view of the other part of the room. Furnishings will also distinguish different parts of the space. A change in wall colour or flooring will instantly make it clear that this area of the room is designed for a different purpose with a different atmosphere.

SPACE-MAKING PRINCIPLES

- Light colours make rooms look bigger.
- Reflective surfaces will multiply the sense of space.
- Plain, unpatterned walls and furnishings look less obtrusive.
- Horizontal lines make spaces look wider.
- Vertical lines make ceilings look higher.
- Small-scale furniture makes spaces look larger.
- Simple window treatments take up less room and admit more light.
- Well-positioned lighting distracts attention from the room's outer edges and focuses attention on the space rather than on its outer limits.

opposite *This narrow kitchen has been created out of a corridor, so, as well as giving cooking and eating space, it links the living space at the front with the bedrooms at the far end. Clever use of mirrors and reflective surfaces widens and enlarges the space.*

right *Plain white walls and an uncluttered window make this tiny bedroom light and airy. Storage is fitted neatly behind sliding doors.*

far right *Large windows and glazed interior doors mean that this house is flooded with natural light. Plain slatted blinds provide shade and privacy.*

practical alterations

Sometimes the only way to get the best from your space is to make structural changes, but these do not necessarily have to be hugely disruptive or expensive. Simply replacing doors or adding a room divider can make a big difference.

Replacing solid doors with glass – or removing them altogether – will increase the amount of light and create views through from room to room (see page 58 for more details). If there is not enough space for doors to open comfortably, you could also consider changing standard hinged doors for sliding panels, which take up less space and add a sleek, streamlined feel. In glass or wood, these too have come a long way since the flimsy hardboard and wobbly tracks that characterized the 1960s obsession with ripping out original features. Now solid and smooth-running, and often full-ceiling height, they are more like an extension of the wall itself than an opening in it.

WORKING WITH WALLS

If you are prepared to put up with more disruption, you could consider removing walls to create an open-plan layout. This will require you to be more disciplined about clutter and storage – open-plan living means not being able to close a convenient door on uncleared dining tables and piles of old newspapers, so it may not be a suitable choice for the chronically untidy. However, having a front door that takes you straight into your living space, or knocking through to the kitchen so that you can talk to your guests while you cook, will change the way you live as well as the layout of your home.

above *Replacing solid doors with toughened glass panels adds a more contemporary look as well as increasing the light flow through the* *house. Modern glazed doors have a smart, industrial edge that combines well with cool colour schemes and minimal furnishings.*

opposite *The neatest sliding doors are more like movable walls, pulling smoothly aside to link adjoining rooms and create more space.*

design options:

STRUCTURAL CONSIDERATIONS

● Any changes you make will need to conform to building regulations. Take a sketch of your plans or the architect's drawings to the local building control department and ask their advice. If other similar houses in your immediate vicinity have already been converted or knocked through, there is a good chance that the buildings inspector will have copies of the relevant plans and know how they are built.

● Your main concern is to make sure that you are not removing a supporting wall. You can usually work out which these are by checking the direction in which the upper floorboards run. The joists will run at right angles to these, and the supporting walls will be at either end of the joists (except around staircases, where boards may have been cut and laid separately from the rest of the floor). Seek professional advice if you are not sure.

● Be careful not to devalue your home by compromising any real historical interest, and bear in mind that you may have difficulty selling it again if you plan any alterations that are too radical or idiosyncratic.

● Some work will be straightforward enough to be carried out by you or by a builder, but for more innovative solutions you may want to consult an architect. This will add considerably to the cost of the project, but it is the best way of making the most imaginative use of the space.

You will find more ideas for space restructuring in the chapters on individual types of room, and additional information about removing doors and walls on page 58.

If removing whole walls is too daunting a prospect, or prevented by structural considerations, you could go for a part-wall alternative. Different heights and layouts will create different effects, and you will probably want to mix walls at a variety of levels to keep the overall feel open and interesting. For instance, you could leave the lower part intact to waist or chest height so that you maintain the sense of demarcation between rooms but create a through view in the upper part.

Also useful, if you have sufficiently high ceilings, are walls that are just taller than adult height, so that they provide effective barriers and privacy between rooms while admitting extra light by leaving the top part of the space completely open plan.

DYNAMIC DIVISIONS

This 'partition' effect is, of course, equally practical if you have a large open-plan space that you want to divide up. Changing your layout can involve adding walls as well as removing them, and introducing a half-height wall is a brilliant way of incorporating a bathing area into a good-sized bedroom, or screening off a work space at the end of a living room.

The other benefit of adding structural layers rather than removing them is that they help to define the existing space. But they do not need to intrude upon it: the trick is to add 'floating' walls that skim the edges of the room but stop slightly short of the basic structure at the sides, ceiling and floor. This supplies a separate plane of colour with clearly defined edges creating shadows and contrasts, so that the wall becomes a feature of the room, not just a background. As a bonus, it can also provide handy recesses in which to position atmospheric lighting.

OPEN-DOOR POLICY

Try to include as many doorways as possible in your layout. They create theatre, opening up views and giving the space a sense of movement rather than establishing a series of dead-ends. Do not feel limited to a standard size: *entrances can be small and slimline, for instance for understairs cloakrooms (think how neatly lavatory doors are designed for aeroplanes), or so wide that it feels as though the whole wall is moving when you open it up.*

opposite *Creating links between rooms helps to establish a sense of the overall space as well as increasing the light flow. If it isn't possible to add a full-size door, internal windows may be an alternative. Here, a window has been installed between the kitchen-dining room and the adjoining sitting room to make the whole space semi-open-plan.*

right *Pillars and columns add structural shape to a space and help to demarcate different areas of use without sealing them off inside separate rooms. Often, all you need is a dividing 'marker' to point out the start of a new area.*

It is one of life's ironies that the space that provides the first impression of where we live so often has the least sense of character and style. Instead of making a statement with the hallway, we tend to present a blank canvas that does not give away too much.

Creating a discreetly elegant entrance is one thing; ending up with something bland and nondescript is less satisfactory. Of course, it must work in sympathy with the rooms that lead off it, but it also needs to establish your style and make the visitor curious about what lies beyond, setting the scene for other furnishings and linking different areas with sureness and confidence. So the look could be bold and intriguing or cool and understated, but what it cannot afford to be is a compromise.

Sometimes there is confusion over whether to treat halls and corridors as part of other rooms or as separate spaces in their own right. Either is fine, as long as you make a decision and stick to it: they only become a problem if you treat them as 'dead' areas and forget to decorate them with the same care as the rest of the home. In many ways, these overlooked spaces actually need more careful thought and planning (even if that is not evident in the finished scheme), especially as they are often dark and cramped, with difficult proportions and not much room to play with. The important thing is to make the space feel furnished, so that it has a life of its own and is not just a corridor to somewhere else.

3 CONNECTING SPACES

establishing
your style

Colour makes an instant impact, so think about the kind of impression you want to create in its application as well as how the hall will link to other rooms beyond. Consider the whole space as part of your plan.

Painting halls and corridors in white is the quickest way to lighten dark passageways and maximize cramped spaces. It is also a neat way of finding out just what space you have got: flooding the whole area with white will give you an effective working canvas to start from. But you may find the effect rather cool and uninviting, when the impression you want to give is one of warmth and welcome. There are several ways round this problem. The simplest is to go for pale shades with a little more depth of colour. Warmer whites, creams and stone or taupe will work if you want to stay neutral, but yellows and pastel shades are a good alternative.

To make more of an impact from the outset, you could go for bolder, richer colours – not so dark that they make the walls feel as if they are closing in on you, but strong enough to fill the space with drama and create a real impression. Reds, gold and glowing jewel colours can work brilliantly if you have the confidence to carry them off. Whether you go for pale or deep colours, though, stick to plain painted walls – patterns are too busy and distracting for the eye to cope with when you are trying to establish a first impression.

LINKING COLOURS

The difficulty with more definite colours is that by giving the hall more of an identity of its own it does not create such a natural link to other rooms. The usual thinking is that a hallway provides neutral territory, unifying different colours by running a single theme along corridors and up stairwells, leading the eye easily from one room to another.

Clever contrasting, though, can maintain a harmonious effect while opening up new colour schemes and giving the whole space more vitality. The trick is to keep to similar tones, such as soft pastels, so that the different colours sit comfortably against one another without clashing because they are all of the same intensity.

EXTRA DAYLIGHT

If a hallway is dark and gloomy, adding a skylight in the roof, if feasible, is a relatively trouble-free way of increasing the light flow down the stairway. Whereas new windows can be structurally problematic and may in fact be prohibited by planning permission, skylights do not affect the building's supporting structure and, because they do not increase the height of the house, will not cause any planning difficulties.

opposite *Painting the different walls of your hall in contrasting but similar-toned colours, such as the pretty, fresh lilac and lemon pairing shown here, will create a harmonious, but dramatic impact that will bring the space to life from the moment that anyone enters it.*

above *One wall of this narrow corridor has been fitted with full-height built-in cupboards to hide the clutter of everyday life (including hats and coats) and present a sleek white surface that reflects as much of the light available in this narrow dark space as possible.*

Think of the hall and each of its adjoining rooms as colours on a palette and make sure that each of them works with all the others, remembering that, when doors are open, all the rooms will be visible at once. You could even paint different walls of the hall in different shades, so that you create different colour combinations from different viewpoints.

FEISTY FLOORING

In a heavy-traffic area like this, flooring needs to be tough and easy to clean. Wood – either polished boards, newly laid blocks or laminates – is one of the easiest choices, and can be continued up the stairs to maintain a unified look. Where space is narrow, try running boards across the width, rather than along the length, to open it up.

Tiles, linoleum and industrial-style rubber will all be practical in a hall, although you will need to find a different surface for the stairs. A hardwearing neutral carpet will work for both, or you could go for one of the tougher natural floorcoverings such as sisal or coir (avoid seagrass, as this has a slightly slippery surface that is not suitable for stairs). Include an area of thick coconut matting, recessed into the flooring, to act as a doormat.

INTRIGUING ILLUMINATION

Keep hall lights soft rather than flooding the whole area, so that you blur the outer edges of the space, which will make the walls recede slightly. Use side-lights and wall-washers to 'brush' a beam against the surfaces, making colours glow and creating interesting shadows. If the ceiling is high, you could also add a flamboyant chandelier fitting or a pendant light hanging on a long lead so that the ceiling is visually lowered and the space feels altogether more in proportion.

Keep doors to other rooms open so that their light floods through to the hall and stairwell during the day. Use the same technique at night, with illuminated rooms visible in the distance, their light and colours adding a sense of space and movement, and leading the eye on to further focal points. Whatever colours you choose for the walls, a large mirror in the hall will make the space feel larger and lighter.

creating viewpoints

Colour and light can work wonders in opening up a warren of dark, dull and cramped spaces. However, sometimes it is better in the long term to take radical action and tackle the problem structurally.

One of the simplest things you can do to increase the sense of space is to remove doors. If you are the sort of person who always leaves them open anyway, because you like the sense of light and the views through from room to room, it is only a small step to remove the doors altogether and make the effect feel more deliberate and permanent.

Alternatively, you can replace solid doors with glass, so that light can flood the interior space instead of being shut off within individual rooms. You do not need to sacrifice privacy: opaque glass will screen off a bathroom or study while maintaining the flow of light through the home. The newest glazed doors are nothing like the traditional, patterned-glass sort: think architect-designed office building, and install a slice of sleek, industrial, sandblasted glass.

OPAQUE PARTITIONS

Take the glass door principle a stage further, and your next option is to replace sections of wall

left *An open-plan space lets you make the most of interesting angles and use the building's architecture to provide its own drama. Here, the line of the staircase adds structure to the room below.*

opposite *This modern open-tread staircase with its curved steel rail provides a feature in its own right, sweeping up gracefully from one floor to the next while giving the hall a contemporary, industrial feel.*

with glass bricks. These can be used either in exterior walls, in effect providing additional windows to let light into the house from the outside, or to lighten interior spaces by removing solid barriers between individual rooms.

You do not need to replace the whole wall: a vertical section two or three bricks wide will have an immediate effect in increasing light flow, as will a horizontal strip a couple of bricks deep towards the top of a wall. Like opaque glass doors, these chunky blocks supply privacy along with light, so they are ideal for screening off areas without blocking the light flow, making the whole space feel far more open plan.

GLASS BRICK CHOICES

These are available in various colours and finishes, and can sometimes be bought from architectural salvage centres as well as building suppliers. They can be installed using different systems – some are mortared in place, while others are slotted into spacers or supplied complete with frames. Some are suitable for exterior use; others for interior projects only, but they may not be load-bearing, so you will need to seek professional advice before installing them.

REMOVING WALLS

The most radical alternative, though, is to remove walls completely, running rooms into one another so that you do away with hallways, landings and corridors altogether to avoid wasting the space on unnecessary 'linking' areas. Where space is at a premium, you cannot afford to have parts of the home that do not earn their keep: a small flat can quite easily lose up to one-third of its space to a corridor, and this would be far better incorporated into other rooms that really need the extra space. At its most efficient, this additional space can be added where it benefits more than a single room at once, so that a run of worktop can be used as an extension of the kitchen in one direction and provide a sitting-room study area in the other.

design options:

MAKING THE HALL FEEL LARGER

- Keep all woodwork and architraving in the hallway as close as you can in tone to the rest of the wall colour, avoiding any over-dramatic contrasts, so that the overall effect is of a single, continuous surface rather than one broken up into several different sections.

- If the ceiling feels too high for the narrow space, balance the proportions by adding a picture rail, then painting the wall above it – and the ceiling between – in a single, lighter colour, so that this area appears larger and makes the corridor feel wider.

- As an interesting alternative to the scheme of using different colours in the same tone, try painting separate walls in varying tones of the same colour, such as taupe and chocolate, or a light blue and a slightly deeper one. This will play with the relative perspective of the surfaces, making some appear to recede while others advance, so that you are able to accentuate the shape of the spaces leading off the hall.

left *Glass bricks and steel stair rails keep this staircase sleek and contemporary and maximize the light available. The green paintwork adds strong colour to make an instant impression.*

exploiting the space

Given the effort you put into squeezing every last inch of space out of other rooms, it is a shame to let valuable spare space in halls, landings and corridors go to waste.

Hallways and corridors are often narrow, and you do not want to obstruct easy access from one room to another, but that does not make them untouchable. In fact, making fuller, more practical use of them will help to bring these 'dead' areas to life and make them feel more like part of the whole space.

PRACTICAL ADDITIONS

One obvious way of exploiting your hallway is to convert the space under the stairs into an extra cloakroom. If you are prepared to install the necessary plumbing, you might also consider a shower room or utility space for a washing machine and a tumble dryer. Remember that where the stairs are at their highest, you may have enough room to stack appliances one on top of the other.

When you are wondering how to use the space, think about the kitchen, too. In an open-plan house, understairs space can provide for a neat run of units and appliances, with full-height walls above on which to fix extra cabinets or shelves, all immediately accessible from the main room but without encroaching on its floor space. And an upper-floor apartment could even fit a narrow galley kitchen along a cul-de-sac landing, with units creating an L-shape between the main wall and the banister rail.

SEATING AREAS

Alternatively, many of these spaces could be supplied with a small sofa or chair, especially if they have a window, making the area a pleasant place to sit. If there is not enough room for free-standing furniture, you could consider building a slim window seat – adding a plain wooden bench with a flat cushion top. This could also contain handy storage underneath. As well as providing

opposite *An entire run of appliances, kitchen units and shelves has been fitted under the staircase to make use of 'dead' space and keep the cooking area away from the main room.*

below *A dressing table and storage chest make use of the landing, adding extra floor space to the attic bedroom and using the natural light from the skylight.*

useful additional seating, it gives the space a sense of purpose, creating points of interest between specific rooms.

DESK SPACE

The key principle is to make sure that you exploit the space under the stairs to its full potential. Unless this has already been boxed in to provide cupboard storage, it is prime territory for creating an extra room and taking the strain off other, overworked areas. If there is no room for an office anywhere else in the house, for instance, this could be an ideal place to establish one. Add a desk or a writing table, and build wall shelves around it to make the space feel more permanent and less improvised.

Ranks of books increasing in height as the stairs rise above them will create a 'furnished' effect as well as being a useful addition to bookcases in other rooms. Fit a good lamp or wall light and the whole place becomes a self-contained home office.

You might be able to achieve the same effect on a landing, too. If there is insufficient space for a full-sized desk, a small writing table will do, providing an extra room en route to the upper floors. Even where the staircase is narrow, you will sometimes find a useful spot where it widens out outside a room, or right at the top where the banister rail meets the stairwell wall and creates an area of wasted floor space beyond access points to other rooms.

EXTRA BOOKSHELVES

You do not need a desk as a reason to install bookshelves. Unless your staircase is very narrow, it is the perfect place to fit extra bookshelves that shave just a few inches off the space. If you are worried about making the stairwell feel too enclosed and oppressive, you could restrict them to the landings, perhaps creating a reading area where you have added a place to sit.

creating an art gallery

One of the quickest ways to make an impression and bring your hall space to life is to use it for displaying pictures and photographs. In this way, a sense of identify will be instantly established which will make the visitor curious about the rooms beyond.

The opportunity of an expanse of uncluttered wallspace along corridors and up staircases is too good to waste, so use it to create a personal gallery of favourite paintings, framed posters and family photographs. It is best to keep the background a plain painted colour: white is the classic art studio look, but stronger colours will provide a dramatic contrast to stark black-and-white photographs, while moody greys will complement contemporary paintings.

right *Turning this staircase into a gallery brings the space to life instantly, adding colour and pattern against the plain white walls and providing points of interest throughout the house. The mixture of different sizes and picture frames keeps the look casual and reinforces a welcoming, informal feel.*

GROUPING PICTURES

You do not need to make the display too formal – what matters is the immediate effect, so colour and position are more important than individual works of art. Grouping them together will ensure that weaker images are carried by the overall impression and turn undistinguished pictures into an intriguing collection.

MAKING PATTERNS

Hanging them in rows or lines can help to balance or adjust the proportions of the space. Pictures hung in vertical lines, like stripes, will make the ceiling look higher, and a dominant image positioned on a far wall – such as the end of a corridor – will appear to advance, making the distant wall seem nearer and the corridor shorter (and therefore wider). Conversely, you could accentuate the length of the passage, making it seem even more like a gallery, by hanging a row of pictures along it. Keep them around eye level and, for a really professional effect, align either the top or the bottom edges of the frames along a single line, so that they appear to be sitting on it or hanging from it.

You could hang pictures on both sides of the corridor, but this might make it feel very narrow and oppressive: it is often better to keep them to one wall, so that they create interest as you pass, while the other wall recedes into the background and makes the area feel more spacious.

CREATING YOUR OWN ARTWORK

If you have not already got a convenient collection of interesting photographs or paintings to hand, you can create your own instant artwork by framing colourful postage stamps, wallpaper swatches or panels of fabric. In fact, some items do not even need to be framed. Small sections of hardboard painted in bold colours can be hung individually or in blocks of four contrasting shades. Use water-based poster or emulsion paint and apply it to the textured side of the

board to give the impression of artists' canvas. Alternatively, you could cover the board with an offcut of vibrant fabric.

DISPLAYING TREASURES

Use the space, too, to display holiday treasures (carvings, shells or coloured glass standing on a narrow shelf against a white wall) or hats on hooks (combining practical storage with innovative display), and include mirrors to increase the sense of light and space. If you have not got a single large mirror, group a cluster of smaller ones to maximize the effect.

above A collection of pictures follows the line of the staircase upwards, with their narrow frames echoing the slim steel handrail. The overall effect is one of cool restraint, with the pictures carefully chosen and positioned for maximum effect rather than clustered randomly together.

storage

If you want to keep your hallway free of clutter, good storage provisions are essential. A suitable place to hang up coats and outdoor clothes is the first thing to consider, but you will also want to provide space for keys, umbrellas, telephones and message books to prevent a jumble of items accumulating day by day.

HANGING SPACE

Hooks and pegs are the simplest way to cater for coat storage, but in a narrow hallway they will quickly block the space, since they are likely to be bulky, so do not site them too near the front door. If there is enough space under the stairs, this is a good site to fix a row of hooks, or you might consider building a wide but shallow cupboard against the hall wall, painted to blend into the wall and with hooks fixed inside. This will keep coats neatly out of the way and, if you fit it with sliding doors, it will not block the hall even when it is open.

If your hall is square rather than long and thin, a traditional alternative that also works well in contemporary settings is a hat stand – a compact unit that will stand neatly in a corner and provide a full circle of multiple hooks at different levels.

Traditional hall stands that combine coat hooks with shelves, drawers and sometimes a mirror tend to look rather heavy and old-fashioned, but you may be able to find a more contemporary design in a lighter, simpler style. Or search for a cheap second-hand piece that could be painted in a pale colour, or in a shade to match the background wall so that it looks like an item of built-in furniture.

TABLES, CUPBOARDS AND SHELVES

Slimline console tables are especially economical on space and are designed to stand flat against the wall – often with a curved front so that there are no protruding corners, and sometimes fashioned with metal plates at the back to screw the table into the wall rather than being completely free-standing. These have just enough room to hold hall essentials such as a telephone, lamp and address book.

If the hall is wide enough, low-level cupboards and shelves will provide very useful storage (for everything from wellington boots to

design options:

opposite *Deep, sombre colours create an alternative entrance, giving an impression of richness and luxury rather than cool freshness. A set of shelves has been built into the cabinet behind the leather seat, providing storage space for practical things like the telephone and a reading lamp as well as display space for decorative items.*

right *Plain white walls help to widen this narrow corridor, and the view of bright bookshelves through the far doorway creates a focal point that brings the room closer.*

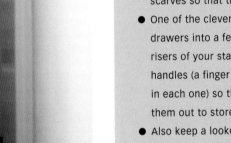

KEEPING THE HALL CLEAR

It is the smaller items that tend to cause clutter in hallways, so provide specific storage to keep them tidy.

- Fix hooks for keys (wall-mounted key cabinets are a useful alternative).
- Use filing trays or baskets to collect and sort mail. To minimize clutter, throw away junk mail immediately, even before you open it.
- Make sure there is a bin of some sort for umbrellas (garden-style urns, for instance, look smart).
- Keep a box or basket handy for things like children's hats, gloves and scarves so that they do not go astray.
- One of the cleverest ideas is to fit drawers into a few of the lower risers of your staircase, with discreet handles (a finger hole is all you need in each one) so that you can pull them out to store shallow items.
- Also keep a lookout for cleverly designed stair baskets, made with a right-angled base so that they slot on to the edge of the step – perfect for gathering up and stylishly storing items left lying around.

spare rubbish bags), while keeping the walls clear so that the space does not feel too enclosed. The top then becomes a ready-made shelf for the telephone, post tray and so on, or, with cushions added, a seat.

If no other practical options present themselves, you could cover a radiator with a smart wooden grille, providing a useful shelf on top, and at the same time smoothing out the wall in a single run of colour.

BICYCLE HOISTS

Where ceilings are high, it is criminal not to make use of the extra space, and in these eco-friendly times, this is one of the best places to keep bicycles. Instead of leaving them outside or letting them clutter up the hall floor, hoist them up out of the way into the space above your head. You can purchase special pulley systems that attach to the ceiling to do the job neatly and efficiently.

stairs and landings

Staircase design has a huge impact on light and space. Where a hall in a single-floor apartment can be moody without feeling oppressive, stairwells need to be opened up so that they create a shaft of light through the home.

Instead of having solid risers, open-tread stairs are horizontal slats supported on either side by the structure of the staircase frame. They increase the light flow considerably by allowing for views through the stairs. If you have a solid staircase, replacing it is a big upheaval, but you might consider adding an open-tread flight to an upper floor if you are planning a loft extension. This would open up the top of the house and make the most of your new windows.

Another option you could think about is to keep the solid-tread stairs but replace sections of the landing floor with metal grilles. These are close-spaced enough to walk on safely and comfortably, but the gaps between the bars will let light flood down through one floor to the next.

HANDRAILS AND BANISTERS

You may not be able to make alterations to the stairs themselves, but just changing the handrails will make a tremendous difference. Chunky wooden banisters are often heavy and old-fashioned – and boxed-in solid sides (the result of DIY alterations in the 1950s and 1960s) make them even worse. To make the whole

right *The elegant tapered sidepieces of this staircase, and the porthole window behind, are slightly reminiscent of a 1930s liner. The whole effect is sleek and graceful.*

effect lighter and more streamlined, replace them with toughened glass clamped to a steel frame, or with steel wire stretched between metal posts. The impression is instantly more contemporary – especially if combined with plain wooden treads – and has a clean, slightly industrial look like an architect's office or an ocean liner.

To emphasize this functional approach, you could also fit central-heating radiators as landing rails (with a separate handgrip running along the top) so that they help to keep the stairwell warm as well as providing a stark modern outline.

If you do not have to worry about child safety, you may be able to do without a handrail. Leaving the stairs open – at least on one side – means that the zigzag pattern of the treads and risers becomes a part of the room's architectural shape (although you may come up against problems with building regulations).

MOVING THE POSITION

Stairs can be rerouted with landings and turns at alternative points, gaining the hallway precious inches. The steeper the stairs, the less space they absorb, and the clearest example of this is a spiral staircase, which takes up minimal room by travelling in a vertical drop. It is not ideal if you have children (and you will have to work out how to get furniture to upper levels), but this is a neat solution where floor space is very limited.

CREATING A STYLE
When decorating the stairs and landing, keep the colours light. Choose a single colour unifying walls and ceilings, and a similar or slightly darker tone for the walls of the stairs themselves.

below *The understairs space in this hallway has been turned into a stylish wine storage area, with a grid of individual bottle slots fitted into the angle under the stairs for quick, easy access from the adjoining kitchen.*

BELOW-STAIRS WINE CELLAR
If the stairs are solid, take the cube storage principle a stage further to fit a whole bank of individual bottle slots, creating a built-in wine cellar. Try a criss-cross network of shelves and uprights, based on one shelf per stair to create a right-angled triangle of storage space.

colours

background walls & wood tones

woodgrain

metal stairposts & accents

foliage & dark accents

green & gold for frames

room recipe:
open staircase

This clever hallway manages to create an open-plan living effect while maintaining a strong sense of vertical space that exaggerates the height of the ceilings and suggests further floors above and below.

WHY IT WORKS:

Instead of individual landings with doors opening into separate rooms, this design uses continuous wooden floors and cut-away white walls to create a unified space where rooms open off the staircase and run seamlessly into one another. The stairs themselves are edged by slim steel posts instead of the more traditional chunky banister rails, so that they recede into the background and yet provide a stark, modern, slightly sculptured look.

Prints and paintings hanging at intervals on the stair walls follow its line, with their shapes and positions carefully chosen to emphasize the high ceilings, contrasting with low side tables and seating units to maximize the effect. The pictures themselves do not need to be modern to suit a contemporary setting. Here, the white background walls create something of the impression of an art gallery or studio, so that paintings of different styles and periods, within a variety of frames, can be hung alongside one another in a random mix, to create an intriguing display in their own right.

This is helped by the lighting. The discreet spotlights are recessed into the high ceilings and fitted in the stairwell so that shafts of light bounce off the walls and illuminate the floors above and below.

The whole effect of a pale, neutral background combined with sleek yet warm wooden floors is comfortable, contemporary and effortlessly good-looking.

KEY INGREDIENTS:

NEUTRAL BACKGROUND
Whites, creams and natural woodwork create a gallery-style backdrop and a unifying link between different floors and rooms.

OPEN-PLAN LAYOUT
Cut-away walls open up views across rooms from the staircase, with slim steel stairposts creating vertical definition and maintaining the open effect.

PLAIN WOOD FLOORS
Stairs and landings are laid with smart natural wood for style and practicality, continuing from room to room to keep the whole space unified.

DISCREET LIGHTING
Recessed ceiling spotlights and wall-washers keep the staircase gently illuminated and define its shape without flooding the whole space too brightly.

PICTURES AND PRINTS
These are positioned to accent the slope of the stairs and provide areas of interest on landings, so that the staircase has a life of its own and is not just a transit area.

When space is short, your living area really needs to earn its keep. You cannot afford to have a room that is kept for visitors only: it has to work hard all day and every day. And it may well have to act as dining room, study and playroom as well as sitting room, so it needs to adapt easily from practical to comfortable, day to night, casual to formal – perhaps with demarcated zones designed for the different activities it has to accommodate. It may even include a kitchen area – if yours does, make sure you plan the two parts of the room together so that they form a cohesive design.

Furniture, fabrics and lighting all need to be thought out with these various uses in mind. You want relaxing colours, comfortable textures and furnishings and flooring that are resilient enough to stand up to constant use. You also need plenty of power points and enough storage to house the different items associated with each activity – books, files, tableware, entertainment equipment. In a room that is used so much, and probably by more than one person at a time, it is easy for things – and furniture – to accumulate, so be doubly strict about clutter control and do not let the household treat it as a general dumping ground.

Keeping a living space comfortable is about maintaining a careful balance between pristine and messy. You want it to feel lived in but not tired out. The best living spaces manage to achieve this look with a sense of effortless welcome.

4 LIVING SPACES

planning the space

below *Frosted glass hides the sitting area but keeps the open-plan feel. Low-level furniture and an informal display of pictures make the setting relaxing.*

However tempting it is to launch straight into designing the ultimate comfort zone, your first move is to think about what other roles the room may need to play. How many people are going to use it, what for and at which times of day?

If your living space is destined to be a multipurpose room, it needs careful planning to get the best out of it. Flexibility is everything. There are two ways to approach this. Firstly, to allocate different parts of the room for different activities, and secondly, to keep the whole area as a unified space but furnish it with dual-purpose furniture that can adapt to different uses at short notice.

ZONING YOUR SPACE

To some extent, the furniture itself will define the purpose of the area – seating, dining table, computer desk and so on. But the distinction between each one can be reinforced by a shift in decorating mood, so that it feels right for the purpose as well as being practically equipped. Painting a couple of walls at one end of the room a richer colour will create a dining area with a sense of drama for evening use, while a corner or alcove could be allocated a different shade for use as a study space. Flooring can signal a change in mood, too, with carpet or natural matting in the sitting area giving way to wooden boards in the dining space.

Furnishing textures will have their own subliminal effect, with fabrics and other soft surfaces automatically denoting comfort, and hard surfaces spelling practicality. But fabrics themselves can divide into simple, robust linens and cottons for daytime and working areas, with more luxurious materials restricted to the comfort zone. And lighting is crucial in establishing and altering atmosphere: make sure you can adjust your lighting levels to create different effects in different areas and at different times of day.

Some rooms lend themselves to being divided up more obviously, with furniture used to form the boundaries of different areas. A sofa positioned at right angles halfway across a long living room will effectively divide the room into sitting and dining areas, while two small sofas at

below *Frosted glass hides the sitting area but keeps the open-plan feel. Low-level furniture and an informal display of pictures make the setting relaxing.*

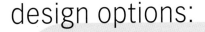

design options:

right angles to each other will create a corner with a protected, enclosed feel. A tall shelving or storage unit standing against the wall at right angles will create the beginning of a partition – just enough to mark the start of a separate area without actually cutting the room in half. For a more emphatic division, you can extend this further, or use folding screens and Japanese-style sliding partitions: these are a neat way of providing instant privacy for a study area.

ADAPTING YOUR FURNITURE

Choose your furniture to match the different roles the room needs to play. A decent-sized table can act as a desk and turn into a dining table when needed. Footstools are useful surfaces for trays and magazines as well as providing extra seating, and ottomans and blanket boxes go one better by supplying handy storage inside for toys, papers and other items. For more organized storage, use the multiple small drawers of classic pharmacist's chests, perfect for filing paperwork and stationery, and providing an extra display surface, too.

Remember that the furniture can be rearranged to demarcate different areas at different times of day or year. A work table can stand under a window during the day, then be moved into the centre of the room for a dinner party. Sofas and chairs arranged round a fireplace during winter months can be regrouped to face the room in the summer. Furniture on wheels is always helpful in a multipurpose room, as it makes rearranging the layout an easier option.

CAREFUL PLANNING

- Plan for the different uses to which the room will be put before you start to decorate and furnish it.
- Think about who is going to use the room and when, and make sure your furnishings will be robust enough to withstand the wear.
- Make sure the lighting is flexible enough to adjust from day to night and between different areas of the space. Fit dimmer switches to vary the level of illumination and add plenty of free-standing lamps so that you can move the focus of light to where it is needed.

left *A folding table maximizes the options for using this space as a dining area or a study. The tabletop can be reduced or enlarged to different sizes, with extra chairs added as necessary according to how it is being used.*

SPACE-MAKING SOLUTION
Make the most of upright chairs: when not in use at the desk or dining table, they create neat side tables which take up far less room than ground-hogging coffee tables.

comfort and colour

Comfort means different things to different people. Some need a living space that feels calm and restful; others need it to be lively and stimulating. The important thing is that the effect can be felt as well as seen: furnishings need to establish the right mood as well as looking good.

MIXING YOUR PALETTE

Neutral colours are always calm and elegant, so a palette of whites, creams, taupes, greys and browns is a classic option for a living room that has to please everyone. Add plenty of warm honeys and browns if the room is dark and receives little daylight, or introduce more grey and stone shades if you want to cool it down.

If you fancy a sense of colour without being overwhelmed by it, pastel shades are restful and understated. Their effect is cool but not cold, so you will get a good sense of space without the starkness of plain white. Soft shades like these will also mix effectively together because of their similarity of tone, so try mixing a pastel palette of accents and contrasts: pale blues, greens and mauves, with touches of pink and creamy yellow to add warmth.

Avoid anything too deep or dark, as it will feel gloomy and oppressive during the daytime. Instead, if you want stronger colour than neutrals or pastels, go for bright, clean shades that feel fresh and stimulating, or for muted colours that have a 'natural' character making them easy to live with: denim blue, earthy ochre and soft moss or leaf green all fall into this category.

LAYERING TEXTURE

Where the colour scheme is restrained, you need plenty of texture to provide warmth, contrast, variety and a subtle degree of pattern. In living rooms, you can build up layers of texture with soft furnishings – rugs, cushions, throws and upholstery all contributing their own element of comfort. Try a streamlined square-cut sofa covered in heavy slubby linen and piled with

cushions in different textures. For good contrast, combine honey-coloured suede, grey flannel, chunky chocolate-brown cord, then complete the look with neat textural detail such as buttoned cushions and blanket-stitch throws.

Look for plain-coloured fabrics that provide their own self-patterning – herringbone woollens, jacquard weaves, corduroy and so on – and adjust the quality and quantity of texture to suit different times of day and year. Add extra layers of warmth and richness in winter, or to boost the comfort factor for evening use; and use fewer layers, in cooler, crisper fabrics, during summer.

SELECTIVE DISPLAY
Be disciplined about individual possessions. Use photographs to establish a personal feel, but do not let them cover every surface: select a group of favourites and turn them into a wall display rather than scattering individual pictures on shelves and tabletops.

design options:

FLOORING SOLUTIONS

Flooring will contribute its own layer of colour and texture. Natural wood – either the original boards or new-laid wood, which can be solid planking, decorative parquet or laminate veneers – always looks smart and creates a feeling of space, while white-painted boards have an attractive modern simplicity.

But these may not provide enough comfort if you are a floor-living person, or have children to consider. Neutral carpet is the soft option, with natural floorcoverings falling somewhere between the two. Be warned: the hardwearing naturals, such as coir and sisal, although quieter than wood, can be even less comfortable because of their rough, hairy finish. However, some of the softer jute and cotton weaves may

not be tough enough for an all-day area. If you want comfort, look for a weave with a high proportion of wool, which will also provide medium resilience.

CAREFREE FURNISHINGS

Remember that comfort is largely to do with peace of mind, so think about practicality as well as aesthetics. If your living space has to suit a busy working or family life, there is no point in going for cream sofas and vaguely hoping they will survive. You need to keep the furnishing fabrics tough and washable. Try traditional denim or drill, or thick linen in mid-tone colours: these will create an understated, contemporary look without showing every mark, and will also be easy to clean when necessary.

DESIGN PRINCIPLES

- Avoid strong colours and busy patterns, as they will not be easy to live with: all-day rooms need to provide a relaxing background.
- If the room is going to have multiple uses, do not go for a dramatic look that is hard to adapt. Keep the overall effect neutral and add luxurious accessories when you want to make more of a splash.
- Remember that a neutral background and flooring will also be easier to work with when the time comes to update the look by adding new furnishings and colours.

opposite *These glowing shades of honey and caramel and rich fabric textures combine to give an effect that is both neutral and warm at the same time. Layering contrasting textures like this is an excellent way to maintain style with comfort.*

left *Cooler shades, like the blues and greens that are used here, will help to open up a small space. Splashes of stronger colour create lively accents against a neutral background and lift the feel of the room.*

planning your seating

Gone, fortunately, is the rigid dictatorship of the three-piece suite, where the sitting area was limited to a semicircle around the television, no matter how badly this arrangement happened to fit the available space.

Today's living areas can be fitted out with individual pieces of furniture in a mixture of sizes and designs, letting you tailor your seating plan to the shape of the room and establish a more personal sense of style. The secret is to aim for low-level seating that will make the ceiling feel higher and the room generally more spacious.

SOFA SHAPES

Sofas are still the most luxurious idea, and you will probably want to include one if you have got room for it, but measure up carefully. Look at different sizes, and do not just go for the biggest one you can fit in the room. In fact, you might find that two small sofas, creating an L-shape or arranged opposite one another, suit the proportions of the room better than a single large one. Supplement sofas with footstools, pouffes or outsize floor cushions if there is not enough space for individual chairs.

left *A mixture of chairs, sofas and floor cushions will give you the option to arrange your seating as best suits the room and the occasion. Keep things as flexible as possible and do not attempt to fill up every available space.*

opposite *Big leather cushions are wonderfully comfortable and can be used as tabletops as well as for seating. Here, they slot neatly under a sturdy, plain wooden shelf unit that can itself provide extra seating when necessary.*

Look out for variations on the basic sofa shape, too. Antique couches, many of them with decorative wooden frames and neat, slightly padded arms, are often smaller and more graceful in design, and create interesting contrasts in modern settings. The classic chaise-longue, with a head-rest at one end and only a rudimentary back support, looks trimmer and lighter than a full-scale sofa (although its position will be limited by which end has the head-rest, so think carefully if you have a choice when you are buying). And elegant daybeds, with frames that sweep up into a curved arm at either end, can stand flat against the wall and be piled with cushions to create a comfortable back.

CHAIRS AND CORNER UNITS

Trend-setters in the 1970s got some things right, one of them being corner sofas. They were popular then because of their compatibility with open-plan homes and are back in fashion now that we have realized how useful they are where space is limited. Low backed and square cut, they will squeeze extra comfort out of wasted corners and, best of all, come as modular units which can build up to whatever shape and size you want.

Do not feel obliged to have a sofa if the room is simply not the right shape. Individual chairs, chosen for their own style and outline, will look more comfortable and have more impact than a sofa that has been forced into a space that is too small for it. Leather chairs are particularly good at holding their own, with a smart, classic look that works well in neutral modern settings. Do not let the effect get too functional and office-like, however, and avoid the Regency study look at the other extreme. The most comfortable and attractive style is squashy and slightly worn – suggesting a practical, hardwearing quality without actually looking antique.

design options:

PLANNING YOUR SEATING

- Do not try to cram too much furniture into the space – if it does not look right, it will not feel comfortable either. You are wiser keeping to a minimal seating layout and supplementing it when needed with chairs requisitioned from other rooms in the home.

- Do not keep adding new pieces just for the sake of change. If you are bored with the furniture you have in place, introduce some variety by creatively adapting what is there – rearranging the layout or changing covers and cushions to suit different seasons or occasions.

- Do not let the television dominate your seating plan – it is invariably in a corner that would not normally create a good focal point. Plan the seating so that it looks right and feels comfortable – considering the positions of windows, doorway and fireplace, if there is one – then put the television in the space that is left. You can always move it – or individual chairs – if necessary when you want to watch it.

eating and entertaining

below *An elegant
pedestal table with
upholstered chairs gives
a 'morning room' effect,
providing a place for
reading during the day
and becoming a dining
area at night.*

If your dining area gets constant use for family meals or entertaining, you can make a clear shift in style to distinguish it from the sitting area. But there is no point in maintaining a dining room if it is only needed occasionally. Better to incorporate it into the main space and create a streamlined link between the areas, then use lighting and furnishing tricks to turn it into a dining room when you need one.

Where space is short, dining tables either need to be compact and unobtrusive or must earn their keep by serving another purpose when not being used for meals. Circular and oval designs often make more efficient use of space than square or rectangular, because they can seat the same number of people without wasting space with jutting-out corners. Tables that can be enlarged when necessary are always useful. A drop-leaf design can be folded to half its size and placed against a wall to act as a desk, then opened out for meals. Some tables have an 'envelope' design that works the opposite way, with flaps that reduce the size by folding up instead of down, so that the tabletop folds inwards on itself and the corners meet in the middle. Others have extra panels that can simply be slotted in to extend the tabletop when the need arises.

Or you could replace a single oblong table with a pair of smaller square ones, using just the one for everyday eating, with the second acting as a side table in the sitting room, then pushing the two together to accommodate more people. This is also a useful option if you have a narrow or awkward doorway that makes access hard for larger pieces of furniture.

TEMPORARY TABLES

A basic work surface such as the classic trestle table is incredibly useful, as it can switch from worktop during the day to dining table at night, and will also fold away for quick storage if you want to reclaim the space. Another option is to keep a separate tabletop that can be laid on top of an existing smaller table to enlarge it for when you are entertaining or for family get-togethers. For this purpose, you could use a sheet of 2cm (¾in) MDF or plywood, appropriately painted or covered with a cloth.

below *An elegant pedestal table with upholstered chairs gives a 'morning room' effect, providing a place for reading during the day and becoming a dining area at night.*

design options:

left Furniture marks out the different areas of this living space, with comfortable chairs set around a large rug and a massive table providing an area for eating and entertaining.

SOFT SEATING

For chairs, you need to decide between upright dining chairs and softer tub or basket shapes. Some of the uprights are a little less straight-up-and-down than they used to be, with streamlined curves, providing a modern functional look in wood or moulded plastic. However, the overall effect is still hard rather than soft. If you want more comfort, add some cushions or opt for the tub shapes with arms and sprung or padded seats, which are more conducive to leisurely meals and relaxed entertaining.

If you need extra seating, use folding chairs that can be stored away out of sight: basic slatted garden or metal bistro designs are stylish and handy, while canvas-slung director's chairs contribute a rather more relaxed feel.

MOOD LIGHTING

Atmospheric lighting is essential for entertaining, as a badly lit table can have a profound effect on our enjoyment. A low-hanging chandelier or candelabra will shed diffused light over the table and create extra shine. Other ceiling-hung lights can be fixed on rise-and-fall mechanisms and wall sconces will provide gentle background illumination. This combination provides a good level of ambient light and enhances the decorative style of the room. Do not underestimate the importance of candlelight, which adds a sense of life and movement as well as a beautifully intimate soft glow. Keep your china plain and pale, and set the table with plenty of glassware (including coloured glass) to reflect the light and increase sparkle.

creating a work space

Work spaces, like dining areas, will probably not need to be in use all the time, so you want to make the most of dual-purpose ideas that let you adapt the room as necessary.

When creating a space to work, the one thing that should really be purpose-built is the seating. If you are going to be sitting at a desk for any length of time, you need a proper office chair ergonomically designed for comfort and support, rather than something borrowed from the kitchen or dining room.

WORKING SURFACES

The most important item is a desktop that is a comfortable height, and good lighting to see what you are doing. You will need a good directional lamp that can focus on your work, and ideally some natural light from a window, too. For a fixed desk, you could consider building a worktop into a corner of the room as part of a run of fitted cupboards. This is a good way of making use of low or sloping ceilings and awkward corners – spaces that are too cramped for most other purposes but fine for one person sitting down. To give yourself the deepest desk space while taking up the least room, fit a worktop right into the corner with a curved front edge to sit at, making it less obtrusive.

Dining tables and trestles are another option, especially folding designs (see page 73). A neat alternative is to fit a tailor-made desktop that folds back against the wall, hinged to a wall-fixed batten so that it can be pulled up (or down) when needed. If you do not want to improvise like this, various purpose-built furniture designs are available which provide organized workspace. Like an updated version of the traditional bureau, these incorporate pull-out shelves to take paperwork or a computer keyboard, and the most impressive of them include filing racks and have fabric-backed pinboard space on the inside of the doors, so that you in effect open up a complete miniature office when you open the cabinet doors.

opposite *The perfect office where space is tight, this cabinet provides a shelf for a computer screen and desk essentials as well as a pullout worktop. Designed rather like a traditional bureau, it incorporates noticeboard space behind the doors.*

right *Equip your desk with storage files and boxes to file papers and reduce clutter. Don't allow your study space to invade the rest of the room: use the furniture to keep it separate.*

PRACTICAL POINTERS

Make sure that you have enough power and telephone points to fulfil all your needs within easy reach of your work area. Look for compact desktop equipment when it comes to equipping your home workstation – choose laptops instead of full-sized computers and combined systems offering, for example, printer/fax/photocopier/scanner all in one, to save on desk space and eliminate trailing wires. Never lose sight of the fact that this is still part of the living space – do not let your work clutter spill over and spoil the relaxed atmosphere of the room.

And, of course, when it is not in use you can neatly close the doors on it as well.

If you have a handy alcove or recess, you can build a series of chunky shelves into it and make the lowest one deeper to create a desktop. This will keep your work space confined in a neat area, and when not needed for work it can be used as an extra shelf or a display surface.

FILING SYSTEMS

To keep paperwork and other office clutter in order, the neatest solutions are all 'closed' storage. Filing cabinets and trolleys can be slotted under your desk, and there is no shortage of handy-sized boxes and files available that can be neatly shelved to present a smart face to the world while hiding all sorts of horrors. Label or colour-code them so that you do not need to ransack the whole lot to find your latest bank statement. Domestic, work and personal papers should be kept separate, and make sure you have

easy-access places for essentials like passports, licences and emergency-repair contact numbers.

As well as ready-made storage systems, you can improvise your own 'files' from everyday containers such as baskets, bins and buckets. Wicker picnic hampers are a useful size for document files and stationery; kitchen cutlery trays and bottle carriers will create neat pen holders; and gleaming galvanized buckets can be used either as smart wastepaper bins or to hold rolled-up plans, sheets of wrapping paper and other larger papers that you do not want to fold.

Make use of wall space, too, with hanging storage on hooks and pegs. A row of square-cut aluminium cans – the sort sold as kitchen containers – fixed to the wall above your desk will hold pens, paperclips and so on. Maps do double duty as decoration and information, and a pinboard fitted into an alcove will provide practical memory prompts for invitations and messages to be answered.

storage and home entertainment

The solution to finding room for your possessions in your living space falls into two categories: hiding things away or putting things on display. There is no simple rule that dictates which is best, or which of the many forms of storage suits which type of object.

Some people enjoy keeping books, CDs and tableware out on show, while others prefer everything behind a slick, streamlined façade of closed doors. The only general guideline is that the less tidy you are by nature, the more hidden storage you will need.

BEHIND CLOSED DOORS

Closed storage is the neatest option. Cupboards, cabinets and drawer units will provide storage slots of different shapes and dimensions, so work out what you need them to hold before you commit yourself to any particular design. You may find individual free-standing pieces that fit the bill, but built-in furniture will make the best use of your space, by taking advantage of the wall height so that it can afford to stay slim-fitting and use up less of the floor area.

Remember that things like books, CDs, DVDs and videos do not need deep storage. The average paperback is only 11cm (4½ in) wide, so you can store masses of these items against a single wall without shaving more than 15cm (6in) off the size of the room. Where you do need deeper storage – for things like vinyl record collections or stacks of tableware – make use of existing recesses by fitting them with shelves and then fronting them with doors to sit level with the adjacent wall or with other built-in cupboards.

If the idea of a whole wall of doors feels too oppressive but you are not tidy enough to trust yourself with open storage, consider partly glazed or frosted glass doors, or line the panels with wire mesh to screen off the contents without obscuring them completely.

Supplement your wall cupboards with floor-level furniture containing hidden storage space. Look for chests and coffee tables that have lift-up lids or integral drawers, or buy individual under-sofa drawers – huge shallow trays on wheels that cleverly slot underneath the sofa, so all that is visible is a wooden panel that appears to be part of the sofa base.

WAREHOUSE-STYLE SHELVES

● If you are not put off by a few rough edges, you can create your own flexible storage system by stacking up wooden crates one on top of another. Make sure they are sturdy and clean, and 'anchor' each one by giving it something heavy to hold (books are ideal). The effect is functional and slightly industrial, with the printed contents or freight details on the timber adding an individual touch. More shallow storage along the same lines can be achieved with planks stacked on bricks, giving a basic, warehouse look that suits simple modern furnishings.

opposite *Built-in storage is one of the neatest options for housing everything from home-entertainment equipment to books. If you need to keep your possessions in order, floor-to-ceiling cupboards could be an instant solution.*

above *These drawers on wheels slide under low tables and shelves to add extra storage where needed. They are ideal for clearing away everyday clutter such as toys and games in a family living area.*

ON DISPLAY

The same principle can be applied to open shelving, with deep shelves built into alcoves (useful for things like televisions and video recorders) and shallow ones fitted against walls. Plan the shelf heights carefully, or use a flexible system that allows you to shift them up and down to different levels, otherwise you will waste a lot of space unnecessarily. Do not assume, for instance, that books all need the same amount of space. Create shelves for different book heights and you will find you can fit two shelves of paperbacks in the same space needed for a single row of illustrated hardbacks.

Cube units provide very effective open storage, with the neat, fitted benefits of built-in furniture yet the flexibility of free-standing pieces, letting you move them where and when you want. They also make excellent room dividers. Arrange your cubes to suit the shape and height of the room: these are particularly useful in attic rooms, as you can create triangular systems under sloping ceilings and fit a run just one or two cubes high where the walls are lowest. Perfect for hi-fi equipment, they will also effectively house photographs, display items, tableware and glasses.

MIXING THE TWO

You do not need to stick rigidly to one approach or the other. Both built-in storage and cube systems can combine open shelving with hidden cupboards to vary the look and give you the best of both worlds. And you can customize your cube system by incorporating smart boxes, baskets and trays. Leave some sections open for display or 'tidy' storage, and then slot in extra containers that can pull out like drawers and store your clutter to keep it organized.

Cleverest of all are systems that hide closed storage behind your open shelves. This will take an expert cabinetmaker, but you can create a

deep layer of spacious storage slots for televisions, hi-fi equipment and files to which you do not need regular access. Then add a set of slim, open bookshelves in front that will pull open like a door to reveal the hidden storage behind.

COMPACT HI-TECH

Home entertainment gadgetry gets a frequent design update simply because it has to keep up with technology. Most developments involve condensing more technology into less space, so the systems are becoming increasingly compact – good news for small living rooms.

Where television cabinets and music centres used to be additional furniture needing as much floor space as an armchair or coffee table, the newest designs – sound systems in particular – can take up less room than a couple of books on your shelf.

Televisions are the bulkiest of the entertainment gadgets, so if you do not want yours to dominate the room, go for a small screen that will fit neatly on a shelf or can be hidden behind a cabinet door. The size quoted is the diagonal width. If you are a film buff and want an image that does justice to wide-screen technology, look for flat screens that do not take up much depth: the latest plasma screens are just a few centimetres or inches thick.

Sound systems have been combining radios, cassette decks and CD players in a single unit for years, with the packages getting progressively smaller and neater and their speakers, once cumbersome boxes needing plenty of floor space to accommodate them, now dainty and shelf-fitting or wall-mountable as wafer-thin panels. The same principle has now been applied to televisions, videos and DVDs, with combined units eliminating the need for several different boxes accumulating masses of trailing cables. Some televisions come with integral video recorders or DVD players; others incorporate DVD player, CD player and radio.

Most larger gadgets come with their own housing, stand or frame, many with a shelf or other integral storage for essentials like discs, tapes and remote controls. Smaller items can be accommodated on shelves or in cupboards, or mounted on adjustable brackets that will swing out of the way when the equipment is not in use.

TECHNO STYLE

The other difference today is that the machinery itself is designed to be put on show rather than encased in cabinet furniture as though we were slightly embarrassed about the workings.

Brushed steel, aluminium and titanium reflect the up-to-the-minute technology and suit sleek modern apartments. Matt black is discreet yet contemporary, and wood veneers and leather-effect finishes add a touch of luxury beyond the purely functional. For a little more fun, you can find systems in bright colours or even with clip-on frames that can be changed to suit your scheme. As a contrast to all that technological wizardry, you can add a dash of classic styling with fashionably retro designs from the 1950s and 1960s, recalling the days when the portable wireless was the height of sophistication.

opposite *Sliding doors are wonderful for saving space, as they don't swing out into the room when pulled open. Here, they are used to hide away books, games and a full-size television screen when not in use.*

right *Dual-purpose cubes provide useful table surfaces as well as spacious storage drawers. Their modular form lets you configure an arrangement that suits your room.*

far right *A storage trolley makes a neat, functional way to file things like CDs and videos. The whole structure is mounted on wheels so that it can be moved out of the way when not in use.*

HIDE AND SEEK

If you can hide the television away, do. It saves space, gets rid of an unwanted focal point and frees you up to arrange the room as you want – you may even find that there is space for an extra chair instead.

colours

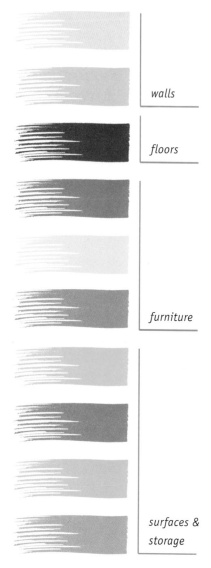

walls

floors

furniture

surfaces & storage

room recipe:
cool sitting room

So many contemporary schemes depend on neutrality for their cool, space-making effect, but this sitting room celebrates colour joyfully, while still keeping its open, spacious feel.

WHY IT WORKS:

The secret here is the pale, pastel shades which reflect maximum light – blues, greens and lilacs, with a hint of soft pink in the background tone adding just enough warmth to prevent the room from feeling cold or unwelcoming.

Combined with these clever colours are neat furniture shapes that leave as much floor space free as possible. The sofa is a simple square-cut design, while the coffee table is small and unobtrusive. The additional seating comprises streamlined upright chairs that stack on top of one another when not in use, and a curved, space-age chair and stool.

The slimline storage cabinets are designed to hold work files and computer equipment against one wall and partially hide it away behind folding doors. Their pale green and lilac colour blends with the rest of the room and prevents the workstation standing out as too functional for this pretty setting. Raising it off the floor increases the space-saving look, as well as leaving room underneath for extra storage boxes, files, trays and so on.

The plain wood floor opens up the whole area and links the pastel sitting room with its adjoining bedroom. Mirrored surfaces, such as the tabletop, increase the light-reflective effect of the colour scheme and, combined with glass vases and other accessories, add touches of sparkle that help bring the room to life.

KEY INGREDIENTS:

COOL PASTEL COLOURS
A blend of pale blues, greens and lilacs reflects the light and maximizes the space.

SPACE-MAKING FURNITURE
Neat, streamlined designs with a slightly space-age feel, using plenty of curves to avoid obstructive corners.

REFLECTIVE SURFACES
Mirrored tabletops and other metals add sparkle and bounce light back into the room.

PLAIN WOOD FLOOR
Polished boards run across the space to widen it and create a sense of continuity with the adjoining room.

PRACTICAL STORAGE
Spacious shelving for books, files, stationery and desk equipment, with doors to screen it when not it use.

room recipe:
warm sitting room

The warmth of this sitting room is evoked partly by its mellow, earthy colours and partly by the intriguing mixture of surfaces and textures that make up its furnishings.

colours

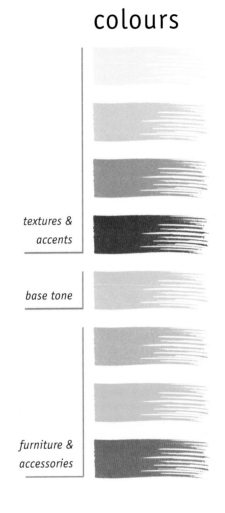

textures & accents

base tone

furniture & accessories

WHY IT WORKS:

The basic coffee-and-cream colour scheme in this sitting room is elegant and contemporary but has none of the cool overtones that such a combination can sometimes evoke. Accents of rich caramel and dark chocolate brown in the cushions and throws add more depth of tone, and the mottled shades of the chimney brickwork extend the basic palette with dull golds and touches of terracotta.

With so much texture and variety of colour, the light, modern wood tones of the table and side cabinet are a neat contrast, and flashes of vibrant blue, in the dish and cupboard door, are clean and refreshing, balancing the warmth of the cream and stone shades without feeling remotely chilly.

The floor is covered with a thick, corded carpet to provide comfort and quiet underfoot and create a warm, inviting setting that is echoed by the soft chairs and big squashy cushions. It is a room to sink into and curl up in, with layers of contrasting fabrics, from flannel and corduroy to fur and suede, providing a rich, sumptuous mix.

The exposed brickwork of the chimney breast supplies additional texture, its artisan-style surface reminiscent of a factory or warehouse, blending utility with simple good looks. The original fireplace has been retained but kept as plain as possible, with no decorative surround to distract attention. The flickering flames become the focal point of the room, enclosed within the circle of comfortable furniture.

KEY INGREDIENTS:

WARM COLOURS
Coffee, cream, caramel and chocolate create a rich, relaxed setting in a range of completely natural tones.

RICH TEXTURES
A variety of surfaces and finishes are provided by the interesting mixture of fabrics, flooring and brickwork.

SQUASHY SEATING
Deep chairs and sofas have plenty of throws and blankets, and big cushions make the floor as inviting as the furniture.

EXPOSED BRICKWORK
This adds to the rich mix of colours and textures, and provides a practical, contemporary feel.

OPEN FIREPLACE
A simple, hole-in-the-wall design with no unnecessary fuss or ornament, just a functional grate for the fire.

The room that is traditionally known as the heart of the home may have to lose some of that status in a compact modern setting. The classic image of a spacious kitchen with a range large enough to bake the week's bread, and a table large enough to seat the extended family for Sunday lunch, was not really conceived with today's streamlined living requirements in view. Small homes are far more likely to have a tiny engine room of a kitchen, just big enough to take the essential appliances, or no separate space at all, just an area allocated at one end of the living room. But there is nothing like lack of space to concentrate the mind on establishing priorities. So start by reducing your wish list to the minimum of essentials, then see how many extras you can fit in on top.

Keen cooks will find all sorts of neat gadgets and space-saving designs to help create a fully equipped centre of operations, while convenience-food aficionados can take advantage of the extra storage for cans and wine bottles. Most fittings and appliances come in slimline sizes especially for small kitchens, and the latest cabinets are designed to streamline the space and minimize obstructions.

It is worth looking at as many different styles as possible, and seeking the professional advice of planning experts, because they will be able to help you squeeze the most efficient use out of whatever room you have available. And because the space is limited, you might find you could afford to have exactly what you want rather than settling for second best.

5 KITCHENS

planning the use

The kitchen is the most practical space in the home, so before you start thinking about which designs and colours you would like – even in advance of measuring up the space – you need to work out exactly what you want from it.

WEAR AND TEAR

Consider how much time you are going to spend in the kitchen, whether it is just for cooking or needs to provide an eating space, too, and what appliances and storage are essential to the way you like to cook. In a small home, the chances are it is more of a pitstop than a centre of operations, with traditional 'family kitchen' activities like meals and homework redistributed to living areas and bedrooms, but it still needs to function efficiently. Some kitchens will have to put up with more knocks than others, so also take into account how many people will regularly be using the room.

Be honest about your cooking capabilities. Do not plan for a mass of appliances you will never use, and think about whether your cupboards really need more space for gadgets or food. Will you want a permanently stocked larder of essential ingredients and exotic extras, or do you buy just what you need for one meal at a time?

Then there is the work surface – do you need enough space to prepare three courses at once and still have room to roll out the pastry, or are you more likely to cook one-pot meals that can be chopped and assembled in very little space?

left *This galley kitchen incorporates an eating area, too, by restricting the fittings to one side so that they don't invade the floor space.*

opposite *This L-shaped layout, highlighted by bright contrasting walls, mixes plain wood cabinets with chrome fittings and appliances for a look that is both modern and mellow.*

design options:

CREATING A DINING AREA

● Small kitchens do not really give you
the option of using them as full-scale
dining rooms, too, but you can still
carve out an eating area big enough
for breakfast or coffee. Circular
tables take up less space than
square designs (little garden tables
are ideal) and a couple of metal-
framed or folding chairs will keep
floor space free.

● If the kitchen adjoins an open-plan
living room, you can extend into it
and create a more spacious dining
area in the border territory between
the two. A kitchen unit or storage
cabinet will act as a boundary if you
want a clear divide between them
(look for curved-end island units to
make the divide slightly softer and
avoid space-wasting jutting corners),
or you could rely on a shift in
decorating style to define the
territory. Changing the floorcovering
from linoleum or aluminium to warm
wood will make the dining area feel
more 'furnished', or you could simply
paint it a different colour.

RETHINKING AND REDESIGNING

Decide whether you want to keep your kitchen as
an entirely separate entity or if it might actually
work better as part of a larger open-plan room.
The great thing about open-plan living is that you
can choose where your boundaries fall, so this is
a brilliant way to steal back a bit of space and
make your kitchen bigger if you feel that you are
going to need it.

If you are planning to redesign the entire
kitchen layout, this is the opportunity to think
about any lighting and plumbing alterations that
would improve its working effectiveness, and if
necessary reposition or add extra power points
to take your appliances.

LAUNDRY LOCATION

*Ask yourself whether you actually need
to do your laundry in the kitchen, too,
or is it practically feasible to install your
washing machine in a separate room?
If you have small children, you may also*
*be reliant on a tumble dryer. Rather
than having two separate appliances
each taking up valuable space in a small
kitchen, it would be preferable to get a
model that combines both.*

planning the layout

Take your time over deciding on the design of your kitchen, thinking through how it will function rather than concentrating purely on the visual effect. It is worth talking to kitchen planning experts to get their advice: most companies offer this as a no-obligation service.

The key thing to remember when planning a kitchen is what kitchen designers usually refer to as the 'work triangle' of oven, sink and refrigerator. These need to be positioned so that moving between them is easy and unobstructed. Site the sink area first because, once you include the draining boards, it is probably going to be the longest unit. (If you want a dishwasher and washing machine, position them near the sink to keep plumbing costs down.) Now plan your food preparation and cooking areas close by. Make sure the hob and oven are only a few steps from the sink so that you do not need to wander around with hot pans. Position the refrigerator near the food-preparation area, but keep it away from the busy traffic around the sink. Try to have work surfaces between all key areas, but keep the main food preparation between hob and sink.

TAILOR-MADE TREATMENT

For kitchens that will only be used by one person, a U-shape or horseshoe layout is ideal. If there is going to be more than one of you in the kitchen, a run of cupboards and fittings creating an open L-shape provides a better layout, so that you have room to get past each other.

Think, too, about individual preferences for height and reach. Decide whether you find drawers or cupboards easier to access (see page 44 for the choices available).

left *Stacking appliances one above another may make them more easily accessible, so plan around the gadgets you use most often. Here, the microwave has been fitted at eye level above the main oven, while the fridge is installed above the freezer.*

left This practical horseshoe layout relies mostly on base units, with the upper walls left clear for hanging utensils. This keeps the effect light and open, while ensuring that all the necessary gadgets are within easy reach. The right-hand worktop also serves to divide the kitchen from the adjoining dining area.

design options:

Plan for ovens, refrigerators and freezers to be at a convenient height: it is usually best to have the oven and refrigerator at eye level, with the freezer lower down as it is used less often. Make sure that worktop and sink levels can be adjusted to suit your height: it is very uncomfortable if they are the wrong level for you, and well-made units will have legs that can be individually adjusted.

ULTRA-SLIMLINE UNITS

The smaller the kitchen, the faster it will be swamped by furniture and fittings. To keep it feeling open and light, find out whether you can have their depth reduced (it is easy to cut a slice off the back of cabinets without affecting the look of the front) or only have floor-standing cabinets and leave the upper walls clear.

WORKTOP LIGHTING

Plan for good lighting to illuminate your worktops. Lights can be fixed beneath wall cabinets so that the fittings do not show, or you could position individual halogen spots in corners for a more sparkling effect. Lights fitted inside

glass wall cupboards will provide a gentle background glow as well as defining the shape of the cabinets, and you can also fit lighting panels to the wall behind a worktop, creating a sort of illuminated splashback.

MEASURING UP FOR CABINETS

Before you start visiting kitchen showrooms and choosing which units you would like to install, you need to know exactly how much room you have available for them. Even if you have decided that your kitchen will be planned by a professional, taking your own measurements and creating an accurate floor plan will give you and the expert planner a much better feel for the project and for what is practically possible.

- Measure the overall dimensions of the room, including the height of the ceiling – many manufacturers produce wall cabinets in a range of different heights.
- Mark fixed features such as doors, windows and skirting boards (including their dimensions), and note the positions of gas, water and electricity supplies.
- Measure any awkward projections such as pipes and gas or electric meters that will need to be avoided. Additionally, you might find it useful to take a photograph for reference, so that you can use this as guidance if and when you visit a kitchen planning company.
- Measure any existing appliances you want to keep, so that you can work them into your plan.
- As a general guide, standard kitchen base units are around 60cm (24in) deep, although there are specialist slimline ones available at 50cm (20in). Wall cabinets are usually about 32cm (13in).

kitchen furniture

The style of your kitchen cabinets will tend to dictate the look of the whole room, because they are likely to cover most of the wall space. Take time to choose the right style, because you will probably spend more on your kitchen than any other room in the home.

Free-standing kitchen furniture is not so dominant, but if you go for fitted cabinets, remember that the style and colour you choose will in effect be your background for all other furnishings and accessories. The key to a modern space-making kitchen is to keep the shapes clean and streamlined, avoiding unnecessary decoration more often associated with old-fashioned country style.

COLOUR AND FINISH

Plain white is always neat, understated and space-making, and is a good choice if you are not sure about your colour scheming plans or need a neutral colour to blend with the rest of the room. White fittings will go with anything and are easy to redecorate around if you want a new look in a few years' time.

Natural wood can look cool and urban, as long as the styling is kept clean and simple: opt for pale woods such as maple, beech and light oak, as dark finishes will appear oppressive in a small space and create a rather traditional effect. Choose flat door fronts or square-cut Shaker-style panels, without any decorative moulding or other ornamentation.

Painted or lacquered wood gives you a chance to indulge in a little colour, with bold primaries adding a dash of cosmopolitan drama and paler pastels doing their bit towards light-reflection and space-creation. Bubblegum pink, banana yellow and that distinctive powder blue all have a fashionable retro feel, reminiscent of American milk bars, and can add a touch of fun to functional fittings and appliances (see page 44). Choose a colour that matches or schemes with adjoining rooms or, if the space is a

design options:

self-contained room, have fun designing a one-off colour scheme by painting individual drawers and cupboards in contrasting harlequin shades.

COOL CABINETS

Natural wood, white and painted wall cabinets can all be fitted with glass fronts as an alternative to solid panels, creating a lighter, more open effect as well as display space for china and glass. Look for industrial-style frosted, textured or steel-reinforced glass. Or go for glass as your core material – cool frosted cupboard

fronts in pale blue or green glass with steel handles are among the most dramatic of contemporary cabinet designs, and can be fitted with interior lighting for even more impact.

SLEEK STEEL

The other material you might want to consider in your kitchen is stainless steel. Already established as the smart option for kitchen appliances, it is now being used for units and cabinet fronts, too, letting you create a whole run of sleek steel for a really professional look.

INSTANT UPDATES

- If the existing units are in good condition and you are happy with the layout, you can save time and effort by updating them rather than ripping them out and starting again. Shabby cabinets can be transformed with a coat of clean colour: use gloss or eggshell for a really smooth surface with a washable finish, or look for specialist melamine paint if your units are made of melamine. Add a couple of coats of good-quality clear varnish for extra protection if the room is a busy family area or subject to lots of wear and tear.

- New door and drawer handles will complete the look: go for unobtrusive metal drawer pulls, long D-shape handles or full-width metal bar grips for the neatest finish, or have fun with coloured glass knobs or pewter-finish designs in distinctive geometric shapes.

- For a total transformation, keep the basic units but remove the original doors and simply attach new ones. Ready-made replacements are available from many manufacturers, giving you a new kitchen without all the hassle of refitting.

opposite *Glass-fronted cabinets can be a good choice – there is no danger of the cabinet doors dominating the room, as can sometimes happen with solid wood furniture. Here, small cabinets and narrow doors add an unusual touch – giving a slightly more traditional look to what is a completely modern kitchen.*

right *The glass fronts of these base units, combined with pale green paintwork and long chrome handles, give a clean, modern effect. A window of glass bricks echoes the frosted glass of the cupboard fronts.*

PRACTICAL ISSUES

The practical design of the cabinets is an important consideration, too – including the mechanics of how they open and close. Normal hinged doors can take up masses of space when fully open, which is a big issue in narrow galleys or U-shaped layouts where an open door can block the whole kitchen. For space-saving solutions, look for doors that fold or slide, either sideways on runners, or upwards on a sash-window principle.

Half-height or split wall cupboards are useful, with doors that swing upwards or fold back into the cupboard recess rather than swinging out into the room.

FREE-STANDING FURNITURE

Do not dismiss free-standing furniture altogether. Free-standing furniture is usually associated with larger, traditional-style kitchens, whereas fitted cabinets can make better use of a small space. However, it can be interesting to include the occasional free-standing piece to give a fitted kitchen a more individual look and added character, particularly if the kitchen adjoins a sitting or dining room that will naturally have a more 'furnished' feel.

If you like the idea of the free-standing look but cannot spare the space, a tall cupboard in the traditional French *armoire* style – like a sort of wardrobe for the kitchen, but fitted with shelves – will be ideal for storing tableware and linens, and make an intriguing contrast with modern fitted units. Or you could include a steel shelf rack or mesh-front metal cupboard for a more industrial feel – rather like an updated version of the traditional meat safe.

CUTTING-EDGE DESIGNS

Some of the up-to-the-minute free-standing pieces are specifically designed to help make limited space work harder. Look out for steel laboratory-style units incorporating a sink and

worktop – and sometimes even a hob, too – which can take the place of a run of units, or provide an island workstation dividing the kitchen from the adjoining space. Some of these units are fitted with cupboards underneath in the same way as standard units. Other types are constructed on legs, thereby creating a more open, spacious effect at the same time as providing room for individual storage crates, trolleys or spare seating underneath.

above This neat cabinet combines cupboard storage and an open shelf in a single wall unit. Beneath it, the brushed-steel worktop and chrome pans add cool, light-reflective surfaces that increase the sense of space.

design options:

right *Assorted storage units provide hiding places for all sorts of kitchen paraphernalia beneath the worktop. The little trolley is particularly useful as it can be wheeled wherever it is needed.*

below *Drawers are often more convenient in a kitchen than cupboards because they give you a clear view of their contents at a glance. Here, the plain white units serve to emphasize the neat, streamlined look of the room.*

SPACE-SAVING TIPS

- Consider installing half-height wall cupboards where ceilings are low, or to prevent the units from dominating the whole room.
- Fit a run of cabinets with an end piece of curved shelves in order to cut off the corner and give a more streamlined look.
- Fit doors and drawers with hidden handgrips so that the sleek run of the unit fronts is not interrupted by knobs and handles.
- Hide appliances behind fascia doors to keep the cabinet lines clean.
- Have the cupboard depth reduced by cutting a bit off the back so that they do not protrude so far into the room.
- Look for doors that fold up and swing back into the cupboard cavity instead of opening outwards.

OFF-THE-PEG OR MADE-TO-MEASURE?

Off-the-peg units can come flat-packed for home assembly or as ready-assembled carcasses. You will be restricted to standard unit sizes, which will probably mean some wasted space in corners. For small kitchens, where precision fit and use of space is a priority, you might prefer to go to a

bespoke or custom-build company, who will design exactly what you want, made to measure. Weigh up the costs carefully. Flat-pack units are much cheaper, but you will have to pay for fitting on top, and you might decide it is worth spending more on a bespoke design with fitting included.

kitchen storage

below *This open storage system looks far less functional than fitted units, and holds kitchen essentials, tableware and display items in chunky deep-set shelves.*

More than is the case with any other room in the modern home, kitchens need clever storage ideas, and contemporary furniture designers are falling over themselves to provide maximum storage in minimum space.

Most storage spaces are built into fitted units, which – for anyone who has more than the barest of essentials to store – are the best way of keeping the kitchen tidy, and will also make the most of 'dead' space that does not normally get used. You can take advantage of plinth drawers fitted into the base of the units at floor level, carousel fittings that revolve to give you access to items stored in awkward corners, plus built-in extras like wine racks, vegetable trays and rubbish bins that would otherwise take up precious worktop or floor space.

CUPBOARDS, DRAWERS AND SHELVES

Some people find drawers easier to access than cupboards and they tend to help you organize your storage more efficiently. Interior trays and dividers will 'file' contents neatly, and different sizes are available to take specific items: extra-deep drawers for pans; miniature spice drawers for small jars and packets.

For the upper wall, cupboards will create a streamlined background but can sometimes feel oppressive in a small space. Open shelves create a lighter effect as long as you can keep them tidy. They are great for displaying china and glass, and for anyone who positively enjoys colour-coding their spice jars and lining up rows of matching containers. Chunky 'floating' wooden shelves, fixed with long screws or bolts so that there is no visible support and painted to match the background wall, will look as though they are part of the fittings. Metal or toughened glass will give a cooler, slightly industrial effect.

TROLLEYS, TRAYS AND CRATES

Supplement fixed drawers with individual containers that can be pushed into spaces beneath tables and worktops or stacked on top of wall cupboards to make the most of high ceilings. Woven-basket or wire-mesh trays become free-range drawers that can be slotted

left *This neat trolley combines a wooden chopping board and knife block with a useful steel tray beneath for storing pans and other essentials. A lighter, movable version of the classic butcher's block, it provides an extra work surface when needed.*

KITCHEN CLUTTER CONTROL

- Reclaim your surfaces. Small-space living is not compatible with the everything-on-show Mediterranean farmhouse look, so lift spice jars and food containers on to shelves or into cupboards to clear your worktops.
- Do not let out-of-date food cans and packets take up unnecessary space. Check your cupboards regularly and throw out anything that is beyond its best-by date.
- Do not let unwashed dishes accumulate. As soon as possible, load them into the dishwasher or wash up and put them away.

left *A steel bar fixed behind the worktop or hob provides handy space to hang gadgets and utensils, allowing fast access for essential tools – making them much easier to find.*

in where needed to store cutlery, mugs or other essentials. Larger steel crates will hold pans, colanders, drainers and so on. And practical trolleys – no relation to the dainty hostess serving tray but more like storage on wheels – can be pushed into position where needed: the most useful of these is the butcher's trolley, which provides an extra worktop and chopping block on top with storage shelves underneath.

RAILS, RACKS AND HOOKS

Hanging storage always helps you save floor and worktop space. A steel rail fixed along the wall behind the worktop, or running along the front of the worktop, can be used to store utensils (with butcher's hooks if necessary), and ceiling-hung racks will store larger items such as pans in wasted overhead space. Wall-fixed hooks and pegs will take individual items from mugs and cheese graters to corkscrews and measuring jugs, and a wall-mounted plate rack will combine storage and draining in one.

DESIGNER DRAWERS

A standard base unit will fit four drawers in the same space occupied by two shelves, and allow you to see what is in them with a clear overhead view instead of forcing you to rummage around to retrieve items buried at the back. Most efficient of all are narrow pull-out units designed like one deep drawer but divided by individual trays or racks inside so that you can see and reach everything from either side. These are available as base units or as full-height cabinets that will fit all your larder supplies behind one slim door front.

walls, worktops and floors

You cannot choose your cabinets in isolation from worktops, splashbacks and other surfaces, so include these in your plans when thinking about colours and materials.

HARD-WORKING BACKDROPS

Painted walls will provide a backdrop for whatever furniture you choose, but you will want to add some sort of protective covering behind worktops and sinks. Ceramic tiles are the traditional splashback material – tough, washable and decoratively versatile. Painted tongue-and-groove wood panelling is a slightly mellower option – neatly nautical (and a good way of covering up a less-than-perfect wall surface) and still washable as long as you use an oil-based paint such as gloss or eggshell. Slate and granite will look smart and dramatic; and newer, more unusual materials include stainless steel, aluminium and heat-resistant glass (available in sheet or tile form) for an urban, industrial look.

CHOOSING WORKTOPS

Worktops can make all the difference to the look of the units – cheap surfaces can downgrade a smart kitchen, while smart choices can make basic furniture look like an expensive designer fit. But you need to think of practicality as well as style: different materials have different merits.

Cheapest are easy-to-clean laminates, available in a huge choice of colours and patterns including imitation marble, slate and granite. But they are not very tough, and cutting directly on to the surface can cause lasting damage. Genuine granite or marble are much more expensive – as is steel – but practical for hob areas as they are hardwearing, resistant to heat and low on maintenance. In a small kitchen, where you are looking at fairly short runs of worktop, it is more feasible to pay for exactly what you want. Granite, slate and marble are also good for pastry making, so you might consider insetting a slab as part of a longer surface.

When it comes to choosing appropriate surfaces for chopping, you are better off with softer, cushioned wood. Look for end-grain blocks, where wood has been turned on its end and glued together, then sliced through into cross sections. These are more resistant to knife damage and are easy to restore if marked, although they can be susceptible to heat and must be regularly oiled to keep them conditioned. Again, wood can be inset as a cutting slab if you do not want a full worktop.

above *Tiny mosaic tiles in turquoise and terracotta create a combined wall and splashback behind this worktop, adding a splash of dramatic colour to contrast with the white work surface and white poured rubber floor.*

design options:

MATERIAL EFFECTS

Try mixing different surfaces to create distinctive effects: for instance, combining industrial steel with mellow wood; or smooth, clear glass with textured slate.

- **Wood** Use it for worktops, chopping blocks and floors. Make sure the surface is sealed and/or oiled to protect the finish.
- **Tiles** Use it for floors, walls and worktops. Colourful but unforgiving, and grouting may get dirty.
- **Glass** Use it for shelves, splashbacks, worktops and even extractor hoods.
- **Metal** Use it for appliances, flooring, cupboard fronts, splashbacks and worktops, plus details like power points, handles and hanging rails. Also try it along the front edge of a plain wooden worktop to give it an industrial edge. It will show marks such as handprints easily and the sheen can be spoilt by limescale if you live in a hard-water area.
- **Granite** Use it for sinks, splashbacks and worktops.
- **Slate** Use it for worktops, splashbacks and floors.
- **Marble** Use it for floors, worktops and pastry boards. Be careful with dark marble which will be marked by acidic substances such as lemon juice, leaving white streaks.
- **Rubber** Use it for floors. Available in sheet or tile form and polyurethane (which is 'poured' into place), it combines a modern, functional look with a warmer texture underfoot.

left Here, the steel of the worktop continues up the wall to provide both a splashback and the housing for the overhead fan. Additional stylish accessories, also in chrome and steel, maintain the modern, light-reflective finish.

Water-resistant oiled hardwood is useful as a soft landing for glass and china around the sink. Stainless steel creates a seamless effect where it adjoins a steel sink, and manmade composites such as Corian or Surell can be moulded to provide a single-piece sink and worktop.

FORGIVING FLOORING

Kitchen flooring needs to be easy to clean, anti-slip and preferably soft enough for dropped tableware to survive the impact. Wood fulfils all these criteria and always looks good. Existing boards (as long as they are in good condition) can be sealed with varnish, or new wood can be laid on top. Vinyl or linoleum (sometimes referred to as Marmoleum) will be softer and (in the case of vinyl) cheaper. Linoleum is harder-wearing and more resilient because it is made from a blend of natural ingredients including cork and linseed oil, which actually gets tougher with age. It also offers you more design choices, including customized patterns cut to match your room.

SURFACE DETAIL

Use your appliances to add another element of style and colour. As well as plain whites, you will find lacquered finishes in bright colours making much more of a statement. Steel, aluminium and chrome, in brushed or polished finishes, give a professional look. And heat-resistant glass can be used for surprising items like extractor hoods, to match glass splashbacks and worktops.

kitchen appliances

Appliances are where you can save an amazing amount of kitchen space, partly by eliminating anything you do not strictly need, and then by choosing slimline, space-making designs for the items you cannot do without.

It is easy to be swayed into including extra features when you are fitting out your kitchen: it is all going on one bill and everything seems so useful that you want to include as many options as possible at the start. But unless you are an aspiring chef, the space will probably be better reserved for storage or work surfaces. Bear in mind that you could probably survive with just a refrigerator and a microwave, then work out your priorities from there.

SIZE AND SCALE

Standard appliances are 60cm (24in) wide, but unless your kitchen needs to service a whole family, the chances are that you do not need the full-sized model and could manage with something smaller. Dishwashers and washing machines are available in 45cm (18in) widths and other sizes, to suit cramped spaces and smaller households. Refrigerators in 55cm (22in) widths and mini refrigerators (equivalent to a hotel room mini-bar) are also an option where room is exceptionally tight.

Cooking hobs do not need to be restricted to the standard four-ring square format. Many manufacturers now make hobs with rings in different configurations to suit individual kitchens, giving you the chance to have just

left *This polypropylene island incorporates a sink, dishwasher and oven behind curved doors designed to take up as little room as possible. The top provides its own cutting surface and internal lighting means that the unit has its own light source for evening use.*

two rings if that is all you need, or a single rectangular cooking zone if it is more versatile for the way you cook. Alternatively, if you have spare a stretch of worktop that is too narrow to take a full-sized hob, you could fit a slimline one with four burners in a single row side by side. Where worktop space is limited, look for a hob with a lid that will fold down to cover the burners when they are not in use.

SMART SINKS

Sinks – the most basic but essential of kitchen fittings – come in all shapes and sizes, including corner sinks to make the most of space that would otherwise go to waste. You can even find miniature versions of the classic butler's sink, giving you the smart square shape and roomy depth but without taking up valuable worktop space. Remember that if you have got a dishwasher, or only wash up small amounts at a time, you will not need so much draining space. A double sink is useful if there is enough room to accommodate it, but look for a design with a chopping board that fits over one bowl to act as an extra work surface.

CLEVER COMBINATIONS

Wherever possible, make use of appliances that combine several functions in one. Washer-dryers will keep laundry space to a minimum and fridge-freezers give you a decent-sized freezing compartment along with your refrigerator. Combination ovens will provide microwave and conventional heating in a single cooker. Among the more recent advances in appliance development are microwave ovens that feature handy toaster slots on the side, together with multi-skilled food processors that will not only cook and steam but even include electronic weighing scales.

One important additional accessory for your cooker is an extractor hood to help reduce condensation and cooking smells. This is really essential if the kitchen is part of or adjoins another room. Most cooker hoods incorporate a useful light, too, and one of the latest designs on the market even combines a cooker hood and microwave oven in one unit.

left *Circular sinks make neat use of difficult corner positions and are useful if you have only minimal washing up. This one is paired with a mixer tap in an elegant arch design.*

design options:

GADGET SENSE

- Avoid buying gadgets and appliances that you do not really need, and get rid of any you are unlikely to use.
- Check for duplicates among kettles, blenders, toasters and so on: choose the smartest and most efficient and dispense with any spares.
- Do not keep gadgets out on the worktop unless you use them regularly: they will just sit in the way collecting dust and require unnecessary cleaning. Store them out of sight until needed.

HIDDEN ASSETS

Where space is really tight – for instance, if you are trying to fit a working kitchen into one corner of a living area – you can get a miniature kitchen which provides all the basic appliances in a single unit or enclosed cupboard. Some are stylish and sleek stainless-steel designs. Sink, refrigerator, draining board with built-in hotplates, grill, microwave and even a dishwasher can be supplied as one dresser-size unit, complete with eye-level cupboards above. Some include built-in ovens and tall fridge-freezer cabinets, and others are designed as triangular modules that will fit into a corner behind neat folding doors.

colours

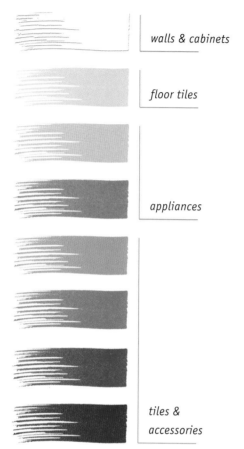

walls & cabinets

floor tiles

appliances

tiles & accessories

room recipe:
simple white kitchen

Built-in storage keeps this all-white kitchen neat and streamlined, with most of the normal clutter hidden away behind closed doors. A few open slots on either side of the cooker are conveniently positioned to hold bottle racks and everyday ingredients.

WHY IT WORKS:

The horseshoe layout of this simple kitchen provides a perfect work triangle so that you can turn easily between the three essential appliances. The cooker is at the far end, twin sinks are on the left-hand run (fitting circular sinks makes it easier to find room for two of them) and the refrigerator is behind a neat cupboard door on the right.

There is enough space on the far wall to fit overhead cabinets without dominating the room. They have been kept fairly shallow so that they do not project too far or obscure the window, and the cabinets themselves are designed as narrow units so that the doors do not swing too far into the room when open.

The worktops have been fitted on two levels, giving the room a more interesting line, and also catering for different working heights, with washing-up and food-preparation surfaces slightly lower than the level of the hob. It is always worth having the cabinet heights adjusted so that the tops are comfortable for your height.

The awkward storage areas in the far corners of this kitchen are dealt with by carousel units and swinging shelves that can be accessed through the side cupboards. The worktops themselves, covered with a mosaic effect, are tough and easy to clean, and add a touch of colour to the otherwise plain white room.

KEY INGREDIENTS:

WHITE CABINETS
The ultimate space-making colour, employed here to open up the small area and keep the room fresh and light.

REFLECTIVE SURFACES
Appliances and door handles in steel and chrome reflect as much light as possible and give the kitchen a sleek, functional modernity.

PRACTICAL WORK TRIANGLE
A neat horseshoe layout creating a practical triangle between cooker, sink and refrigerator.

PLENTY OF STORAGE
A full range of floor and wall units keep the room neat, and include a few open slots for faster access.

SPACE-SAVING CABINETS
Slimline wall units are designed with narrow fronts to accommodate storage more efficiently and remain unobtrusive.

The bedroom is the one place where you can afford to indulge your creative decorating instincts without restraint. This is private space that does not need to keep the rest of the world happy 24 hours a day, so you can choose colours purely to please yourself and design tailor-made storage to suit your clothing.

The atmosphere you create is up to you. You could go for luxury and decadence, with rich fabrics and sumptuous textures; or for calm sophistication, defined by elegant tailored lines and cool, neutral colours; or perhaps the refreshing simplicity of painted floors and furniture and crisp gingham covers. The trick is to devise a room where you feel completely at ease – a retreat from the rest of the world where you can switch off and totally relax.

But you need to think practically in order to establish this impression of effortless calm in a limited space. Your bed is a priority, as it needs to combine comfort with style: use linens and covers as key elements in your furnishing scheme rather than purely functional fabrics, and choose a bed design that does not swamp the proportions of the room. Efficient storage is crucial to keep your clothes organized and leave the space free of clutter, and lighting must be soft and subtle to establish a mood of calm. Exploit the full ceiling height and take advantage of clever ideas such as gallery beds that free up the floor space and platform beds that incorporate built-in storage. And look for additional places that will accommodate spare sleeping spaces and concealed guest beds.

6 SLEEPING SPACES

planning your sleeping space

below *Built-in hanging space is an alternative to a wardrobe with doors in this atmospheric bedroom. Shelves set above and below offer additional storage.*

For bedrooms to provide the restful space you need for sleep, they must be clutter-free. That means clothes put away, the floor clear of books and shoes and not letting the casual layering of bed linen degenerate into a tousled muddle.

CREATING CALM

Feng shui principles go so far as to dictate that bedrooms should be used for sleep and nothing else: that you should not keep books here, or have a study area or have clothes out on show. In particular, outdoor clothes should not be visible, as these distract you from the inward calm of rest and sleep.

This approach may be a little extreme for some, but you can see the point. Where space is limited, it is all the more important that the 'sleep centre' takes precedence.

The paradox is that, to get your sleep centre right, you need to make good storage a priority, so that you keep clothes, footwear and accessories out of the way and leave the floor clear for the bed. Do not automatically buy a massive wardrobe if most of your clothes do not need full-length hanging room: it will be wasted on separates and shirts that only take up half the space. Work out whether your clothes need shelf, drawer or hanging storage, allocate space accordingly (see page 118 for practical storage ideas and fittings) and stick to the system – do not let things stray.

If possible, position the bed where you can walk freely all the way round it and do not have to climb over it to reach essential items. Where space is really tight, in attic bedrooms or beneath awkward ceilings, fit the bed where the height is lowest. This space will not be much use for storage but is fine where you will only be lying down, and can create a cosier, safer-feeling place in which to lay your head.

design options:

SCREENS AND PARTITIONS

One way of keeping the bed area separate and clutter-free is to create a floating wall that divides the bed from storage or other furniture. This need not take up much space – it simply gives the bed a sort of extra-high, free-standing headboard, pulling it forwards into the room rather than standing it against a structural wall. The extra space behind the bed can then be used for storage or a dressing room. So although it reduces the floor space that the bed stands in, it makes the area look bigger by freeing it up from other furniture. If you do not want to construct a fixed wall, you could achieve the same effect with a free-standing screen behind the bed.

If the bedroom adjoins your bathroom, it might even be worth merging the two and reallocating the space, using a floating wall to replace the existing structural divide. This can give you the chance to absorb wasted corridor or landing space, as well as creating the luxury of having a bathroom virtually in your bedroom.

PROPORTION AND SCALE

To create a light and airy impression, make sure that any peripheral furniture is small and neat in design. Slim console tables – the sort designed to stand against a hall wall without obstructing the space – can take the place of full-sized dressing tables, and bedside tables only really need to be big enough for a lamp, clock and perhaps a separate radio to stand on. A pair of small tables, or even stools, one on each side of the bed, will actually take up less space than one larger bedside table.

The one item that is worth having as big as possible in the bedroom is a mirror. As well as providing that all-important clothing check, it will reflect the available light and make the whole room feel twice the size. You do not even have to bother about fixing it in place on a wall – a huge mirror leaning casually against the wall looks wonderfully decadent and makes you feel as though you are in control of the room, rather than being restricted by it.

BEDROOM CLUTTER CONTROL

- Always put clothes away when you take them off, or put them in a linen basket or laundry bag ready to wash.
- Throw away clothes that no longer fit you, that you regret having bought, that are marked or damaged beyond practical use or that are no longer in fashion (you can keep the occasional favourite for fancy-dress parties, but not the whole lot). Do not hold on to them on the basis that you paid for them and want to get your money's worth – better to cut your losses and get rid of the guilty irritation you feel every time you see them.
- Do not allow magazines and books to accumulate by the bed. Recycle, file or return them to the bookshelves.

right *The curved screen in the foreground creates an elegant partition to divide the sleeping area from the living space in this open-plan apartment.*

far right *Plain white bedlinen, textured covers and additional cushions combine calm with luxury and help turn the bedroom into a sanctuary.*

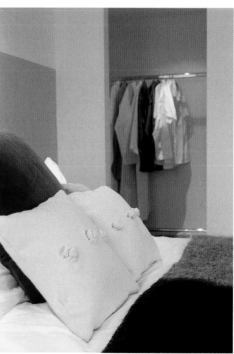

colour and texture

Colour is a crucial element in a bedroom – you need to choose shades that will be gentle and relaxing at night and, if the room is likely to be used at all during the day, refreshing and comfortable in natural light, too.

Soft blues, greens and mauves are cool and restful; pinks and yellows will add more warmth if you want it; creams and whites are unfailingly calming and elegant. When used on bedroom walls, all these colours will help to open up a small room and make it feel more spacious. Bear in mind, though, that there is no innate need for bedrooms to be airy. A small room has the advantage of feeling warm and protective, and if you want to accentuate this womb-like effect, you could opt for bright, rich or deep shades that surround you with more definite colour.

LAYERED LINENS

The beauty of bedrooms is that they automatically provide masses of fabrics with which to build up your colour scheme, giving you

the opportunity to layer subtly varying shades for a richer, more textured effect, while they literally add texture with their contrasting surfaces. Crisp white linen or fine Egyptian cotton are classic and simple, with extra decoration such as embroidery or jacquard-weave patterns providing more detail if that is to your taste. Creams and whites, as ever, enrich each other if layered

LOW LIGHTING

Lighting needs to be kept subtle and atmospheric – you are aiming for mood here, not practicality. Fit dimmer switches to keep levels soft and adaptable, and use individual lamps to diffuse the light source and accent individual areas rather than flooding the whole room, providing illumination where you want it for reading, make-up and so on. If you have built-in cupboards, consider fitting interior lights (in heat-resistant casings) which will make it easier to track down specific items.

below *Pure white is always restful, and here provides a zen-like calm in this very minimalist bedroom, in which all of the clothes storage is hidden neatly away behind closed doors.*

above *A colour scheme of white and pale lilac is restful and romantic for a bedroom, blending contemporary style with a touch of tradition to make the most of the space and the light from the deep sash windows.*

single colour or pattern. But the contemporary revival of classic sheets and blankets, appreciated by designers for their more elegant lines, has restored a sense of real pleasure in the way beds are dressed. Simple layers of white linen and grey wool blankets will achieve this in tailored, understated style – far neater in a small room than a bulky duvet. Alternatively, for sheer luxury – and to help you forget that your space is in limited supply – indulge in an extravagant collection of contrasting fabrics and varied textures. For instance, combine the elegant drape of heavy woven blankets with sensuous silk eiderdowns, then add deep piles of different-sized cushions and pillows on top.

BAREFOOT COMFORT

A neutral-coloured carpet, or a natural floor covering in cotton, linen, wool or jute, will be soft and warming under bare feet and will make the most of the floor space. Wood looks good in bedrooms, too – especially white-painted floorboards, giving a simple, scrubbed, utility effect that succeeds in opening up the space and reflects the practical and relaxing qualities that the room needs to balance.

THE SPARKLE FACTOR

With so much light-absorbent texture around, the room can feel slightly muffled by fabric, so try to incorporate a few reflective surfaces to catch the light and bring the space to life. Mixing silks and satins among your bedlinens will help, as will mirrors. Metal-framed furniture, lamps and frames provide a reflective gleam, and the glass droplets of chandelier light fittings will add a more decorative sense of sparkle.

Flat wall colour can be enlivened by painting the woodwork and any cupboards in eggshell paint, which has a slight sheen to it. You could even cover one wall or a chimney breast with painted wood panelling to extend this effect over a larger area of the room.

together, and ginghams, chambray or plain-coloured cottons will mix comfortably with them. Plain linens in coffee, stone and grey add a cooler, more sophisticated look that always suits contemporary homes.

The wholesale adoption of the duvet has rather drained bedlinen of its traditional character, with those shapeless quilts swamping the entire bed in an ungainly, lumpy layer of

RESTFUL WINDOWS

Keep the colour of your curtains or blinds similar to the walls, so that you do not get jarring blocks of sudden colour or pattern at the windows. Curtains will be more often drawn here than in daytime rooms, and a dominant

fabric that provides an attractive frame for the window when drawn back or rolled up may look overpowering when opened out in larger panels. It is usually more restful to surround yourself with a single sweep of colour.

bed styles and shapes

The style of the bed itself will make all the difference to the look of the room. You can choose to dominate the space with a scene-stealing centrepiece or go for something more discreet that blends into the background.

Comfort is paramount but the style can create a host of different effects.

The simpler the bed, the less space it will appear to take up. If you want to maximize the space or need to fit in other furniture such as a writing desk or dressing table, look for streamlined beds without head- or footboards to get in the way. Simple frames, though, can add a sense of style without overwhelming the room. Plain metal frames with barred ends, like classic hospital or school dormitory beds, are a neat alternative to the traditional high brass bedstead. Look for painted metal or brushed steel rather than the bright polished finish, to keep the effect understated and contemporary.

Wood sounds a mellower note, warmer than metal but still keeping the look practical. Avoid shiny orange pine (which always looks uncomfortably bright and is especially harsh in bedrooms) and steer clear of decorative carving and turning on the endboards and posts, or the room will lose its modern edge and lapse into something more like traditional country style. Aim for light wood and simple, square-cut designs to maintain the streamlined look.

DARING DECADENCE

It is sometimes more fun, though, in a room that is your own personal space and where you can decorate to please yourself, to splash out on something more dramatic in style. Again, this will convey that you are not going to be limited by the space. Wooden sleighbeds, with endpieces carved into gentle curves faintly reminiscent of a traditional sleigh, have a classic elegance that does not fight with contemporary furnishings. The wood is usually dark, which may look rather heavy and oppressive in a small room, but if you paint it a light colour, it will instantly appear smaller and less obtrusive.

Decorative metal looks elegant and romantic, with a delicate framework that will suit a small space as long as it is painted in a light colour.

design options:

CHOOSING THE RIGHT BED

- Always try beds out in the shop to test the mattress for comfort.
- Arm yourself with accurate measurements, including doorway and staircase dimensions, to make sure that you will actually be able to get it into the room.
- Where access space is tight, look for hinged bed designs that fold in half, or that come in two halves and can be bolted together in situ.
- Map out the bed size on the floor of the room to gauge accurately what it will look like and make sure there is enough space to walk around it. Even if it fits, it may overwhelm the space visually, so you might want to opt for a slightly smaller size to keep the room in proportion.

Or you could go for leather, one of the smartest new looks around: a plain headboard in soft, matt leather combines a streamlined simplicity with an irresistible sense of luxury.

For a real flourish, and to turn the bedroom into a cocoon of comfort, add still more fabric and dress the bed with its own curtains. Gauzy white muslin is a brilliant way of casting a feeling of romance over the setting without swamping the room completely. A ceiling-fixed mosquito net is the simplest way to achieve this effect, but for more drama, and to screen off the bed from distracting storage or work areas, create a contemporary four-poster. Forget any visions of overblown flounces and heavy drapes. With a frame in plain unadorned metal or wood, and sheer cotton muslin curtains, this looks wonderfully romantic and restful.

above *A solid wooden base supplies this bed with deep storage drawers underneath as well as creating a built-in headboard that acts as a shelf.*

UNDER-BED STORAGE

If you are short of storage, bed bases with deep drawers built into them are extremely useful for holding spare bedlinen, or for clothes like jumpers and T-shirts that do not need hanging.

Alternatively, look for a bedframe with plenty of space beneath it and add separate wheeled drawers like shallow trolleys that can be pushed under and pulled out with ease.

extra sleeping space

If you have a boxroom or study that you want to turn into an occasional sleeping space, or you live in a studio apartment and want the daytime effect to be of a sitting room rather than a bedroom, look for clever beds that can be neatly hidden away when not in use.

The most practical of these are the ones that masquerade as something else during the day. Sofabeds turn sitting space into instant bedrooms (look for a design with a properly sprung mattress if it is going to get regular use), and Japanese-style futons provide basic low-level seating on a slatted wooden base that will fold out to a double or single bed. You can also find double-layer divan beds that are a neat size to act as a makeshift sofa in a study. The lower mattress slides sideways and upwards to sit level with the upper one and double its size to make a bed. And specialist companies are designing all kinds of 'instant' bed options, with mattresses that can unfold from boxes and beanbags wherever you need them.

FOLD-UP BEDDING

For studio rooms, the neatest idea is a bed that folds up into the wall and is disguised as a cupboard front during the day. These can accommodate full-sized, fully sprung mattresses, comfortable and supportive enough to be slept on every night, and will incorporate the bedding, too, so there is no need for you to remake it each time. You simply pull the cupboard open and the bed is there ready to be slept in. As an inventive

USE-ASSESSMENT

When choosing or designing extra sleeping space, think about how often it will be used. For regular use, you need a simple mechanism and comfortable mattress. For occasional use, you can put up with a thinner mattress and any extra hassle in getting it made up ready for use.

opposite This clever gallery bed folds down from the top of what appears to be a huge cupboard, to provide a spacious sleeping area. Ladder rungs up one side of the structure provide access to the platform without taking up any extra room.

right The inside of the platform structure has been fitted with clothes storage, so the room could be used as a studio or bedsit or for occasional overnight guests. The cupboard door slides neatly to one side to take up as little room as possible.

For rooms with high ceilings, you can go one better and raise the bed on to a gallery with open space below. If you are lucky, you may be able to keep this above head height so that it does not restrict your use of floor space at all. At the very least, you will be able to fit a work table or some kind of seating here. Gallery beds are really the adult equivalent of bunk beds (you never quite lose the childhood excitement of climbing a ladder to bed), and if you can fit a narrow couch or sofa beneath the gallery, you are virtually reproducing the bunk-bed principle and providing two beds in one.

Bear in mind that you can create a gallery sleeping space in any room with a high-enough ceiling: the concept is not confined to the bedroom. A small galley kitchen at one end of a sitting room may have a lot of wasted overhead space, and you could put that to good use by fitting a false ceiling and slotting a mattress on to the extra floor area that it provides. Similarly, bathrooms do not need high ceilings, so you could add a lower ceiling and use the space above it to create a separate sleeping platform, with ladder access either from the landing or from an adjacent bedroom.

alternative, the bed can be fitted sideways and folded up against the wall, so that the wooden sidepiece of the frame forms a useful shelf at around dado-rail height.

PLATFORMS AND GALLERIES

Where you want to combine somewhere to sleep with extra storage or work space, one of the most efficient ways is to think vertically and install the bed at a higher level, freeing up the floor area beneath it for another purpose.

If storage is your priority, consider putting the bed on a platform: building a deep cupboard, low wardrobe or set of drawers against the wall with a top large and robust enough to form the base for a mattress. Run a ladder up one end of the platform to give you access to the bed without obstructing the drawers or cupboard doors.

BUILDING A GALLERY BED
Creating a gallery is probably a professional carpentry project, as it needs to be secure enough to hold both mattress and sleepers and to provide a stable access ladder. You might also want a rail along the front edge, particularly if the ceiling is high enough to allow you to stand up in the gallery space rather than just crawling into bed.

bedroom storage

Most of your bedroom storage will be for clothes, but you may also need to house dressing-table accessories, toiletries, make-up and so on. And, unless you are abiding by feng shui principles, you may need space for books and mementos.

Following the same principle described for storage in living spaces (see page 82), you first have to distinguish between items for display and those for concealment. How many of your possessions can stay out on show and how much room do you need to hide things away?

BESPOKE SYSTEMS

As in living spaces, closed storage will help keep the room clutter-free and, once again, the most efficient system is to build it in to create customized spaces for different kinds of item – in effect, taking the principle of the fitted kitchen and applying it to the bedroom. Fitted-bedroom companies have perfected this as an art form, and it is worth looking at the gadgets and tricks that they employ to find a place for everything, even if you do not want to buy their cabinets. The key is to create several individual compartments behind your closed doors rather than one long hanging space, giving you the flexibility to treat each section independently and devise different storage systems for each one.

First work out how many of your clothes need to be hung rather than folded, then divide hanging clothes into full length and half length. Dresses, coats and long skirts need full-length space, so one section of your cupboards will

left *This sophisticated scheme of creams and chocolate-browns is calm and restful. Simple shelving maintains this effect, with a few carefully chosen items on display against the plain, painted walls and bedroom clutter hidden away in deep drawers fitted under the bed.*

design options:

DOUBLE-DEPTH CUPBOARDS

- If you have two bedrooms linked by a partition wall, you can 'pool' their storage space by replacing the wall with a deep layer of cupboards, in effect creating a double wall with a storage cavity between them. This lets you give each room a double-depth cupboard, each one using up the full depth of the wall space but only half its length, so that the two cupboards sit side by side but face in opposite directions, like the storage equivalent of a loveseat.

- You also have the perfect opportunity to create a 'shared' closet with access from both rooms. Leave one end of the wall free of cupboard fittings but fix a door on both sides so that you can walk through from one room to the other. This area can then be equipped with a rail running the full depth of the double wall and will provide ample hanging space.

right *Calm need not preclude entertainment. For the ultimate in relaxation, this sleek, oriental-style run of cupboards incorporates a television hidden behind a mirrored panel. The mirror slides up to reveal the screen, which can be operated from the bed opposite.*

need to be fitted with a high rail for these. Shirts, trousers, skirts and jackets need only half the length, so you can save space in another section either by fixing two rails, one above the other to create double-decker storage, or by fixing one high rail and then fitting cupboards or shelves beneath them.

The rest of the space can be taken up with shelves and drawers in different sizes and depths. Fit extra-deep drawers for jumpers, with smaller, shallower ones for things like underwear and socks. Look out for transparent drawers in wire or acrylic which let you see their contents without too much rummaging. Make use of high-level shelves to store items not needed so often. Then take advantage of additional ideas that are designed to be slotted into larger systems to help keep things neat. Racks fixed to the inside of the door will hold items like scarves and ties;

honeycomb organizers can be fitted inside drawers to 'file' small items individually; shoe racks will stand in the bottom of the cupboard to keep pairs together without scuffing; and shoe hangers provide a strip of open-sided canvas 'cubes', each one taking a single pair. Incorporating a few deep shelves will also give you space to stack boxes and baskets commandeered as improvised 'drawers' (see page 120 for more ideas).

SPACE-SAVING DOORS

Where space is tight, you do not want to obstruct it with cupboard doors. Consider fitting sliding doors rather than hinged ones, so that they do not swing out into the room. In a very small space, it helps if the doors are also mirrored, to increase the amount of light and make the room appear twice as large.

extra storage ideas

There are masses of additional storage devices to help keep bedroom paraphernalia out of the way and turn your room into a stress-free space for relaxation and sleep.

Look for free-standing chests fitted with extra-deep drawers designed to hold jumpers, and deep-drawer trolleys that can be pushed into place wherever you need them. Or improvise the same effect with an office filing cabinet painted in bright enamel paint.

Big laundry baskets – reminiscent of out-size picnic hampers – and wooden blanket boxes will hold spare bedlinen and bulky sweaters, and additionally provide a useful table surface or window seat on top. A collection of hampers or old, characterful leather suitcases stacked stagecoach-style in descending order can be used to hold out-of-season clothes or other items not used regularly, creating a smart display in an alcove or corner.

left *Hampers and suitcases stacked against a wall will provide plenty of extra storage for crush-proof clothes and accessories. Here, they fit neatly into the space between the window and the sliding cupboard doors, using up a run of wall not wide enough for any other purpose.*

opposite *This cupboard shows how efficient planning will make room for different types of clothes storage. The rail provides full-length hanging space, with shelves fitted above to take jumpers, T-shirts and other accessories. Box storage on the top shelf holds gloves, scarves and jewellery.*

design options:

Smaller boxes are perfect for storing scarves, gloves, undies, belts and jewellery. Look for decorative hat boxes that will sit on a chest of drawers or in a disused fireplace, and Shaker boxes, traditionally made from thin layers of cherry wood curved round into an oval shape. On a more prosaic level, salvage and cover shoe and boot boxes with fabric or paper, to fit under the bed, on top of cupboards and in shelf units.

LATERAL THINKING

Make use of storage not specifically designed for clothes or bedrooms. Pharmacy chests and kitchen spice chests provide useful little drawers for items that would easily get lost in a larger space. Modern stationery shops stock all sorts of miniature filing cabinets, originally intended for desk essentials but perfect for things like jewellery and hair accessories. Vegetable racks can slot inside cupboards to hold foldable clothes, and old-fashioned bicycle baskets, with one usefully flat side, can be strapped on to a tie rack on the inside of a cupboard door.

CREATIVE HANGING

Additional hanging storage can be supplied by free-standing clothes rails on wheels, the sort you always see being whisked around on behind-the-scenes shots of fashion shows. And as an alternative to the full-sized wardrobe, canvas-sided designs that close with zips or fabric ties are a good temporary measure, as they can be collapsed and folded away when not in use.

Hanging storage is particularly useful if it keeps floor space clear, so look for sets of fabric pockets that will hang inside a cupboard or on the back of a door to hold shoes, socks or underwear. A peg rail or row of hooks fixed to the wall in traditional school-cloakroom style will keep belts, scarves and hats neatly lined up, or can be used for drawstring bags to hold laundry and clothing accessories.

ON SHOW

Open shelves keep things more colourful, so you could stack T-shirts and jumpers in colour-coordinated ranks like a shop display, but you will need to be scrupulous about folding them, cleaning them regularly and guarding against moths which like nothing better than a soft pile of woollens to munch through.

HEADBOARD SHELVES

- Give a plain divan bed a custom-made headboard and you can provide yourself with a bedside shelf at the same time. The trick is to build a slimline cupboard out of MDF and attach it to the wall behind the bed.
- Make the cupboard about 15cm (6in) deep, 1m (3ft) high and a little wider than your bed. Design the cupboard with end panels that open to let you slot flat items inside the headboard, such as pictures that you have no room to hang, artwork and document portfolios and so on.
- This also gives you a shelf above the bed for books, photographs, radio and reading light, and eliminates the need for a bedside table if floor space is in short supply.

TAILOR-MADE STORAGE

Coats really need to be hung on well-padded hangers to keep their shape. Hanging them by a skimpy collar loop will simply drag the fabric and gradually spoil the line of the tailoring. But an even better proposition is a proper dressmaker's dummy, complete with life-sized curves so that it provides coat

storage and an innovative sculptural display all in one. Unfortunately, the classic solid wood models are rarely found nowadays, but simpler versions with cotton stretched over a basic frame are more common, or you could use a shop-window dummy made from moulded plastic or clear perspex.

colours

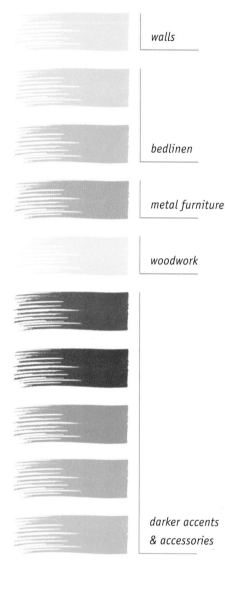

walls

bedlinen

metal furniture

woodwork

darker accents
& accessories

room recipe:
space-making bedroom

Furniture is of paramount importance in a bedroom, as it is all too easy to clutter up the space with heavy, oppressive pieces. This bedroom solves the problem by concentrating on sleek, reflective steel frames and open-work designs.

WHY IT WORKS:

The furniture shapes are all simple – a dormitory-style bed with plain metal head- and footboards, and chunky wall shelves with no visible brackets or supports. This keeps the overall effect clean, contemporary and space-saving, and also lets you incorporate larger items (the wide bed; a spacious desk) without things looking too bulky.

Colour makes a bedroom feel more comfortable and lived-in, and is especially important if the room will be used during the day, like this room with its neat work area. Cool and restful, the pale blue and green create a feeling of space and reflect light. They also mix well together: blue adds a crisper note to green, which can feel slightly institutional on its own, while the natural 'organic' quality of green takes the chilly edge off plain blue, so that the resulting mix is gentle but not too flowery.

Crisp white blinds and paintwork offset these pastel shades, and the bedlinen adds a subtle element of pattern, mixing different designs without looking too busy. The soft, impressionist flower motif scattered across the duvet cover blends perfectly with simple plaid pillows in the same colours and yet contrasts with layers of plain white cotton.

This is a very effective mix of soft, pretty colours with cool modern surfaces and accessories – the perfect balance for a contemporary bedroom.

KEY INGREDIENTS:

LIGHT BLUES AND GREENS
A cool, fresh colour scheme that opens up the space and reflects maximum light. Restful and gentle for a peaceful bedroom setting.

REFLECTIVE SURFACES
Steel-framed furniture, lamps and other accessories to maintain the cool theme and bounce light back into the room.

PALE WOOD
Desk and shelves in a light, receding, pinkish wood tone that blends into the pastel colour scheme instead of dominating the room.

CLEAN MODERN SHAPES
Streamlined furniture designs and simple chunky shelving keeps the whole effect understated and contemporary, free from any fuss or frills.

PLAIN WHITE ROLLER BLINDS
A neat finish to the windows, providing privacy without blocking too much light, and keeping fabric to a minimum rather than swathing the glass with flouncy curtains.

room recipe:
cosy bedroom

colours

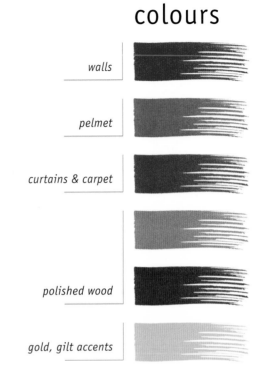

walls

pelmet

curtains & carpet

polished wood

gold, gilt accents

Sometimes it can be effective to vary the mood of your colour scheming and go for something completely different. This rich, womb-like bedroom provides a dramatic alternative to the usual cool, pale colours and space-making furniture.

WHY IT WORKS:

Include a room like this as a one-off indulgence in a modern setting, and you will find its distinctive style adds a touch of vitality to all that understated elegance. The key ingredient is the colour, which accentuates the restricted space rather than trying to open it up. All rich colours are enclosing and protective, but warm reds, golds and oranges are the most effective. Here, the result is made all the more cosy by fitting the bed into a neat recess. The arched enclosure and pictures on the walls make this space almost a room within a room, but the white ceiling prevents it from feeling too claustrophobic.

Plain white bedlinen is cool, crisp and timelessly classic, so there is no chance of this setting looking fusty or old-fashioned, especially when it is combined with the moody charcoal grey of the pelmet, which adds a distinctly contemporary touch.

The faintly Baroque-style drama is maintained by adding rich polished wood, such as walnut or mahogany, instead of pale ash or beech, and trimming the room with decorative gilt accessories such as lampshades and mirrors, instead of cooler, more modern chrome or steel. The result is warm and inviting, with soft carpet adding comfort and sound absorbency, creating a cosy retreat that is perfect for curling up in.

KEY INGREDIENTS:

RICH RED WALLS
A warm, dramatic scheme that encloses the space to make it feel more intimate.

ARCHED RECESS
Fitting the bed in here increases the enclosed feel, and is a neat way of making use of a potentially difficult architectural feature.

CRISP WHITE LINEN
The classic choice for bedrooms of any style, and the quickest way to refresh a tired-looking furnishing scheme.

GILDED ACCESSORIES
Used sparingly to add a touch of opulence and continue the richness of the colour scheme. Look out for sheets of gold leaf and gilding cream, from craft or artists' supply shops, to let you add gold highlights to plain surfaces.

POLISHED FURNITURE
This picks up the rich colour and adds sparkling reflections. Try cherry wood, which has a bright, glowing tone, or classic leather with a polished chestnut finish.

A priority for many, while a mere practicality for others, the bathroom is one of those rooms where decorating is a daunting prospect. Either you know what you would like but are not confident about achieving it, or the space is so difficult that just fitting everything in is a challenge.

Usually small, often windowless and with plumbing and pipework to work around, bathrooms often get left at a compromise stage simply because the idea of ripping everything out and starting again is too intimidating. Really, though, they should be incorporated into your plans for the home right from the beginning, because what you do with the bathroom can affect other rooms, too. You may need space for a washing machine here, for instance, if there is not enough room in the kitchen or utility room; or you might decide to do without a lavatory in the bathroom if there is a separate one elsewhere in the house.

Contemporary furniture makes a big difference to bathroom layout: bath shapes and sizes are far more flexible than they once were, and basins come in shallow, streamlined, semi-transparent designs that barely seem to take up any room at all. So by going for a completely new set of fittings, you can use the space far more efficiently, making the room feel bigger or even shaving off wasted inches so that they can be put to better use in an adjoining room. The trick is to accept the inevitability of a short period of upheaval, and free up your mind to think clearly about how you want your new bathroom to work.

7 BATHROOMS

bathroom priorities

below *White tiles and fittings make space in this tiny bathroom. A mirrored panel increases the space, and a lavatory is hidden behind a frosted glass door.*

Now that an all-mod-cons bathroom is an accepted part of a working house, we have all started to expect more of this little room, looking for luxury and indulgence over and above smooth-running practicality.

The demanding pace of contemporary life means that we crave a sanctuary in which to retreat, and the rise of single-person households gives many of us an opportunity to spend more time in the bathroom rather than fighting for a ten-minute slot before bedtime.

Look at newly built homes and you will see that they recognize these changes in our lifestyle and society by paying far more attention to the size and layout of the bathroom, incorporating second bath or shower rooms and en-suite washing facilities where possible, and creating better access from other bedrooms. You may not have quite so much flexibility if you are redesigning an existing dwelling, but it is worth using the same principles to devise a room that suits the way you live.

ASSESSING YOUR OPTIONS

Start by working out what you need from your bathroom – and what you can quite happily live without. There is, for instance, no law dictating the gold-standard installation of a full-sized bath, separate shower cubicle, basin, lavatory and bidet in every bathroom. It may be a dream layout in the sort of hotel suite where the bathroom is as big as the average sitting room, but it simply is not necessary if you prefer showering to bathing anyway, have a separate toilet down the corridor and only use the bidet for washing your underwear.

You could be much better off by fitting a full-strength power shower in a luxury cubicle, doing without a bath and bidet and using the extra space for a built-in airing cupboard, a linen cabinet for spare towels and bedding or even a washing machine and tumble dryer. On the other hand, if the bath is an indulgence you cannot do without, make it a priority to choose the most comfortable size (see page 132 for more information on different styles and shapes) and be prepared to sacrifice the bidet or some of your storage space to make room for it.

design options:

HOW MUCH PRIVACY?

Privacy is another important issue to consider. A single person may be happy with an open-plan layout where the bathroom is simply a walk-in area adjoining the bedroom. Or for the ultimate indulgence (and if you have space), you could install a free-standing bath in the bedroom and turn the whole room into a sybaritic retreat. Family homes, though, will probably require proper doors and enclosed shower cubicles, and you will need to think about the best position as well as appropriate access points. If the room has enough free wall space, it might be feasible to plan for access from two separate bedrooms on either side of it.

In all bathrooms, even open-plan designs, it is worth creating private areas with partitions so that the main washbasin area can be used while the shower and loo are screened from view, making the room more practical for use by more than one person at a time. These can be built as tiled or glass-brick partitions, or created with panels of frosted or sandblasted glass, providing a ready-made shower screen without the need for a separate enclosure. Part walls like this can also house plumbing, letting you position a toilet or basin against it and free up existing wall space for other fittings. Or you could simply fix ceiling-hung bamboo blinds that can be lowered when you want to divide up the room Oriental-style.

BATHROOM CLUTTER CONTROL

● Bathrooms are invariably on the small side, so you need to be especially strict about keeping clutter under control. Whether you are aiming for streamlined practicality or a luxury retreat, unwanted items will interfere with the purpose and spoil the effect.

● Plan plenty of storage, either built-in or with a range of attractive free-standing containers.

● Be ruthless about throwing out non-essential equipment or accessories.

● Pack away spare toiletries until they are needed.

● Throw away old or unused cosmetics. If you have not used them before now, you are never going to. They gradually deteriorate anyway, so impose a six-month shelf life and get rid of anything that is out of date.

left *Blue walls are always cool and refreshing. Here, a half wall forms a neat shower enclosure and the short bath helps to make the most of the space. A circular mirror echoes the shape of the porthole window.*

bathroom layouts

Unlike living and sleeping areas equipped with free-standing furniture, bathrooms do not let you rearrange the layout when you feel like a change, so you need to try to get it right first time. You can always introduce new accessories if you want to update the look.

PLANNING ON PAPER

Use the grid system explained on page 16 to draw up a floor plan and try out the fittings you want to include in different positions until you are happy with the effect. Take a look at the bathroom furniture designs on the following pages to get an idea of the different shapes and sizes available, including pieces specifically and often ingeniously designed to fit into corners or other small spaces.

Do not automatically position the bath along the longest wall. A slightly shorter design may well fit across a shorter wall instead and leave you with more free floor space. Other useful positions for baths are against walls with windows (the bath will fit beneath the window, whereas a basin or lavatory cistern might be a problem) and beneath sloping ceilings (where there is insufficient space to stand at full height but plenty of room to lie down).

Bear in mind that doors and windows can be moved if necessary to improve the layout. A doorway repositioned across the corner of a bathroom will leave you with more usable wall space for essential fittings. And if the bathroom is under the roof, you might consider installing skylight windows and blocking up an existing window to provide extra wall space.

If you are short of wall space on which to hang radiators, think about installing plinth heaters instead in the base panels of fitted furniture. Keep the bathroom floor and other surfaces clear wherever possible. Look for wall-hung furniture and fittings, and take advantage of any space-saving accessories such as wall-mounted soap dispensers.

right In this innovative layout, the bath has been fitted diagonally into a corner, with taps installed in a separate, free-standing column. The streamlined curves and mosaic tiles suit the restricted space to keep the whole effect neat.

opposite Wall-hung fittings keep the floor space clear, and a simple glass panel divides the lavatory from the shower area. A tall ladder radiator provides sleek towel storage.

FITTING IN FURNITURE

Bathrooms can be fitted with cabinet furniture on the same basis as kitchens, with streamlined units housing the various 'appliances' and offering useful storage in the spaces between them. Tailor-made floor-to-ceiling units, incorporating just one or two panels of open shelving, will provide a particularly sleek and stylish solution, although at a relatively high cost. Alternatively, you could build cabinets around individual items: washbasins in particular benefit from cupboard housings that readily turn them into vanity units, which provide a handy surface for lotions and potions around the sink as well as additional storage space neatly tucked away behind closed doors below.

If the room has any useful alcoves or recesses, make the most of these, too. A toilet or basin can be positioned in a recess and the space above it fitted with a series of shelves to hold towels or toiletries.

USING SCREENS

If you are planning to divide the room with screens for privacy (see page 129), their positions need to be taken into account at the planning stage. A shower or lavatory, for instance, could be sited at the far end of the bathroom, with a partition built out at right angles to screen it. If there is enough available space, you could install both fittings like this, on opposite walls, each of them screened off from the rest of the room. This also has the advantageous effect of giving the main room additional wall space, against which you can site the bath or washbasin.

DOOR SPACE

Check how much space is taken up by the door when it opens into the room: you could free up wall and floor space by rehanging it so that it opens outwards instead, or by replacing it with a sliding design.

design options:

PLUMBING AND PIPEWORK

- Installing a new bathroom suite will be a relatively uncomplicated and inexpensive process if you are happy to stick with the position of the existing fittings. The pipework is already in place, so all you need to do is plumb in a new bath, basin, lavatory and so on.

- To make the most of a small room, though, you may well find the best solution is to rearrange things, and this is when extra pipework becomes necessary, so be prepared for extra expense and upheaval.

- Moving a lavatory will involve running an internal pipe to the external position of the soil pipe or repositioning the soil pipe.

- Adding a shower, either over the bath or in a separate cubicle, will mean new pipework, plus connection to the electricity supply if the shower is a powered model.

- Bear in mind that if you are going to end up with ugly internal pipework, it could be a good idea to install fitted furniture that will hide it all away behind neat panels and inside cupboard units.

furniture and fittings

Bathroom fittings are increasingly designed with limited space in mind, with ingenious ideas to save inches and make use of wasted corners. Look for furniture that leaves floor space free, so the whole impression is larger and less cluttered.

BESPOKE BATHS

You do not need to give up on the idea of a classic bath that is long enough to stretch out in. Try out slightly shorter lengths – unless you are very tall, you will actually find shorter baths more comfortable because they provide a foothold, letting you relax totally without fear of drowning. Or look for tapered designs that narrow at one end to save space. Corner baths are still a practical option as long as you go for plain white rather than caramel or avocado, which are too reminiscent of the 1970s. Install them in a smart tiled or neat wood-panelled unit rather than a moulded plastic shell.

Half-length baths fit into very tight spaces. They are usually extra deep and incorporate a ledge seat, so that you can still submerge yourself without having to stretch right out. The latest take on these are square tubs, often with wooden surrounds conjuring up a minimal Japanese or Scandinavian effect, a cool blend of utilitarian function and designer style. But bear in mind that if you scale down other fittings, you can afford to be more indulgent in your choice of bath: leave out the bidet and sacrifice the shower cubicle, and you could find you have room for a free-standing roll-top as a luxurious centrepiece.

INNOVATIVE BASINS

Washbasins have completely reinvented themselves in the last few years, so take inspiration from the innovative effects you see in designer restaurant cloakrooms and explore showrooms and catalogues for a full range of styles. The classic ceramic pedestal basin resting on a floor-standing column is still available, and you will find small sizes to suit cramped conditions, but the pedestal does waste unnecessary floor space.

It is worth looking at basins that come as an integral vanity unit instead. They take the same amount of floor space, but you gain a lot of storage with it. And think about the way

design options:

opposite Restricted bathroom space need not prevent you from indulging in luxurious fittings. Here, a decision was made to get rid of the bidet and provide space for a deep roll-top bath to give the room a sense of opulence.

right This circular steel washbasin design uses several space-saving devices. The basin itself is small and compact, while the soap dish is wall-mounted, and the taps are fitted into a wall panel.

SPACE-SAVING SOLUTIONS

- Make sure you eliminate any moulded plastic bath panels, which tend to be bulky and obtrusive as well as distinctly unattractive. Replace them with a flat surface – tiled or painted MDF, sandblasted glass, plain wood or neat tongue-and-groove panelling.
- If you box in the bath behind any sort of fixed panelling, check that you can open it again to access pipework when necessary for dealing with repairs and emergencies.
- Look for wall-mounted taps to match your fittings: having the handles fixed to the wall above the bath or basin keeps the surround free for storing toiletries. The mechanism will take up about 8cm (3in) of concealed depth behind the wall.

bathrooms are designed in train and boat cabins – fitting the basin into a built-in countertop gives you a storage surface for toiletries as well as hiding away ugly pipework.

Even more efficient in their use of space are wall-hung designs, where the basin is suspended on brackets and pipework diverted into the wall to keep the floor below clear. In fact, if the floor space is freed up, you can get away with a larger basin because the overall effect is less cluttered and more spacious.

SURFACE INTEREST

It is the materials, though, that have made the biggest difference to modern basin design, and opened the way for sleek new shapes. Glass (chunky and textured like ice, or frosted and opaque) and stainless steel will both create shallow, elegant 'dishes' that can be wall-mounted on brackets or can sit on countertops. These are the best for saving space, as the curves are streamlined, with no intrusive corners. If you have slightly more room, robust materials like stone and marble create a more down-to-earth look, but still conjure up imaginative effects such as circular 'tub' sinks or deep butler's-style troughs, like a smaller version of the traditional kitchen scullery sink.

COMPACT LAVATORIES

Like basins, these are neatest when they are wall-hung, so that there is no pedestal cluttering up the floor, and the cistern is concealed behind the wall. Some are designed to fit right into corners; others to protrude as little as 50cm (20in) into the room. If you fit a floor-standing lavatory, it might be a good idea to look for a two-piece circular pan (originally a Victorian design, but still made by some specialist companies), so that the wastepipe link can be swivelled to the best position before the two parts are cemented together – really useful if you are trying to fit the lavatory into an awkward space.

SHOWER SPACES

Showers, now that the technology is so advanced, are increasingly desirable as the most refreshing, water-efficient and space-saving way of washing. Powerful pump-driven showers can be fitted over a bath (so that they do not take up any extra room), in very restricted spaces such as under the stairs, in the corner of a bedroom or as part of a small en-suite. They can even, if necessary, take the place of the bath altogether in the main bathroom.

If you do not want to give up your bath, you have the option of fitting it with an overbath shower or installing a specially designed shower bath, which is shaped with an integral shower tray at one end to create a larger area to stand in. If you can find the space, though, a separate cubicle is more satisfactory – partly because it allows the bath and shower to be used at the same time, and also because the latest cubicles are now being designed with luxury extras such as body and steam jets.

You need to allow a square metre (yard) for the average-sized floor tray, and make sure there is enough space around it to allow you to get in and out of the enclosure easily. Corner cubicles are a neat way of maximizing your floor space.

OPEN OPTIONS

In many ways, it is better not to enclose the shower at all. When the bathroom is already small, there is something rather perverse about building an even smaller room inside it.

above *This tidy little bathroom shows how a short bath can be fitted across the width of the room, to make the best use of the space. Extra storage has been built in under the washbasin.*

Instead, leave the cubicle open, so that it has sides to contain the water jet (best tiled floor-to-ceiling for maximum water resistance), but no door boxing it off. If you do want to create a screen for privacy, the best curtains are double-sided, with a waterproof liner on the inside and a fabric outer layer in towelling or smart textured waffle, to soften the clinical edge.

Most luxurious of all is the Continental-European-style 'wet room', where the whole space is tiled, and water simply flows away through a drain in the floor. This is still a relatively new idea in the UK, because it involves the devising of safe water drainage for predominantly timber-framed houses. However, designers are already coming up with ways to solve the problem, for instance by setting an aluminium tray into the floor beneath the tiling, so it is worth thinking about. If you do opt for an open shower, remember to install effective storage for towels and toilet rolls, otherwise these will get drenched along with the rest of the room.

left *The most satisfying design for a shower is the fully tiled 'wet room'. Here, the circular shower is built in a combination of mosaic tiles and glass bricks, with the drain creating a central motif in the pattern of the floor.*

colour and surfaces

below *Glass tiles give this bathroom wall a glowing, light-reflective finish. The cool aqua tiles have a translucent, jewel-like surface that creates subtle shifts in colour and suits the watery setting. A glass shelf emphasizes the reflective quality of the tiles.*

All the rules about white being a good colour for small spaces become loaded with extra significance when it comes to the bathroom. White is the *only* colour for sanitary ware, whatever size the room may be.

Every now and then the bathroom designers try to reintroduce subtle shades of cream or pink (usually referred to as champagne) for baths and basins, but it is not the same. White is clean, classic and – unless you have decided to splash out on a material like marble or stone instead of traditional porcelain and cast iron – it simply feels the most natural choice for bathroom fittings. It will never date (white fittings are sought-after at architectural salvage centres in a way that aqua and burgundy never will be, except in a post-ironic fantasy sense) and when the time comes to sell your home, you will find it far easier with a white bathroom suite.

COLOUR SCHEMING

Because bathrooms tend to be small, a palette of pale, light shades is a good idea for the rest of the decorating, too, but here is where you might want to deviate from bright white and add a stronger element of colour or character. As well as choosing colours that will open up the space, you can create very different effects and alter the mood of the room. Richer, creamy whites used for walls or tiles will look elegant and throw the white sanitary ware into sparkling relief; deeper contemporary neutrals such as stone and taupe will add a Zen-like natural calm; cool blues, greens and mauves will reflect the room's watery associations; soft plaster pinks will add warmth, and give you the chance to create a more luxurious, boudoir look if you have had enough of all that understated minimalism.

WALL PROTECTION

A mixture of paint and tiles is the simplest choice for bathroom walls. If the room is well-ventilated, you could opt for a specialist wallcovering, but you will need to apply it with a fungicide-containing paste, and patterns are not a good idea in a small room anyway. Look for emulsion paint specially formulated for bathrooms so that it will resist mould and damp. If you are interested in authentic architectural materials, it might also be worth considering limewash, which can be mixed with pigments to different colours. This will need to be applied over lime plaster or brick (you cannot paint it over modern emulsion), but it responds well to damp environments without blistering or developing mould.

CHOOSING TILES

You will want tiles to create a protective splashback around the bath, behind the basin and to line shower cubicles, but hesitate before tiling the entire bathroom from floor to ceiling. A vast expanse of tiles can be overpowering in a small room: patterns will confuse the eye, and even plain tiles can be surprisingly uncomfortable, creating a rather clinical effect in a restricted environment – more like a hospital than a sanctuary.

To avoid this, it might be worth looking at the new generation of natural-finish tiles, which present a matt surface recreating limestone, slate or alabaster rather than the high gloss of traditional glazed tiles. Glazed surfaces are useful for their reflective finish, which acts almost like a mirror in bouncing light back into the room and helping to open up a small space, but the effect can be fairly easily overdone, creating too prominent a glare. So matt tiles are an effective compromise, combining practical water resistance and plain colour with a more subtle, comfortable finish.

Mosaic effects, created from hundreds of tiny tile chips, are always intriguing and can sometimes work in small rooms, where their 'miniature' nature seems appropriate for the proportions. But again, be careful not to overdo and in consequence spoil the effect: it will be accentuated by the confined space, and therefore may be better limited to a single wall or shower lining rather than covering the whole room.

Other types of tile worthy of consideration in the bathroom are glass and lustred tiles. These are not to be confused with the chunky glass bricks used for partitions and interior walls, but are delicate wall tiles with either a clear, jewel-like glow or an iridescent mother-of-pearl finish. These provide a glorious range of colours and subtly shifting shades, with a gently reflective surface that provides a light-enhancing gleam rather than a bright shine.

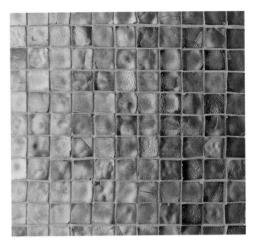

right *Tiny mosaic tiles with an iridescent mother-of-pearl finish create a soft gleam in delicate colours. A mix of blues and lilacs will catch the light and help to increase the sense of space in a bathroom.*

left *A wide shelf around the bath gives storage for toiletries as well as adding a sense of luxury. The central tap fitting means that the bath can be used from either end. The circular washbasin saves space and has no sharp square corners to protrude into the room.*

TURNING UP THE HEAT

Bathroom heaters are part of the furniture these days, with sleek designs and contemporary colours contributing as much to the look of the room as the suite and tiles you choose. If you have wall space to spare, fit a ladder design that will double as a towel rail. Where wall space is limited, extra-narrow radiators can be fitted into narrow strips between appliances or beside the frame, or look for floor-level cylindrical designs that run along a skirting board and pump out ample heat from a compact shape. The chunky scale of old-school-style pillar radiators would normally be too big for a small bathroom, but you will find new versions with a reduced number of pillars and sometimes an integral towel rail, too, bringing this classic design right up to date.

right *A mellow, organic colour scheme makes this small bathroom ultra-relaxing. The basic palette of moss green and natural taupe creates contrasting tiled surfaces, while the plain white porcelain of the fittings adds a crisp, fresh note. Towels in golden ochre and rich chocolate-brown contribute a warmer feel that offsets the expanse of tiles, which could otherwise look rather cold and clinical.*

design options:

UNDERFOOT ISSUES

The bathroom floor needs to balance aesthetics with practicality – you can bend some of the rules if the space will be used just by one or two adults, whereas a busy family bathroom will need a more rigorous approach. Ceramic tiles, along with stone and marble, look smart and are waterproof and easy to clean, but they may feel cold and hard underfoot and are inclined to get slippery when wet.

If you want a little more comfort, or have children to worry about, you will need to add washable cotton rugs or go for a softer option altogether. Wood has a practical appeal that looks good and suits the clean lines of contemporary style while adding a mellower note, but floorboards will need to be well sealed (or painted) to make them waterproof, and you need to be careful with laminates, which have a tendency to warp and lift if subjected to constant damp. You may find sheet vinyl a better option (this is easy to lay, and can imitate almost any look you want, from wood to stone or marble). Alternatively, you could go for something uncompromisingly modern such as rubber, which is warm, waterproof and incredibly hardwearing. Avoid linoleum, however, as it simply will not

stand up to the high humidity. Bear in mind that you can always add wooden slatted duckboards to give a vinyl floor a more utilitarian look, or to provide a safe, non-slip surface on top of marble or ceramic tiles.

ADDING WARMTH AND TEXTURE

Glass, mirror, chrome and ceramics are the key elements of any bathroom – hard, cold, reflective surfaces that are practical and generally useful for opening up the space, but not terribly inviting or comfortable for a room in which you want to be able to linger and relax. You now need to add softer materials that balance the chill and contribute warmth.

The most obvious of these ameliorating elements are bathroom linens: piles of towels in thick fluffy cotton or, for a slightly more sophisticated, urban look, in textured waffle. Classic white linens are always the simplest and soundest, but you can select other shades to adapt the room's colour scheme.

You might also want to incorporate areas of plain wood, for bath surrounds and fitted furniture: the mellow finish of beech and cedar adds a smart Continental-European-style simplicity to contemporary bathrooms.

SIMPLE SOLUTIONS

- If you are fortunate enough to have a window in your bathroom, do not swamp it in unnecessary fabric. Instead, obscure the glass with a frosted or sandblasted design for privacy, or add a simple blind that will screen the window without blocking the light.
- Do not break up surfaces with too many patterns or changes of colour and texture. Choose one colour, or similar tones, for the walls and ceiling, and keep your tiles and floor design unfussy.
- Use reflective surfaces like chrome, stainless steel, glass and large mirrors to lighten, open up and magnify the space.
- Fit halogen lights to add sparkle and 'lift' an enclosed area. A scattering of recessed ceiling spotlights, combined with good mirror lighting, will make the room feel much more spacious.

left *This wall-mounted basin picks up the design trends coming through in some smart restaurant cloakrooms. The high fitting provides a built-in splashback, and the taps are positioned in a vertical line to one side, above the soap rack. It is a compact, modern design that combines style with function very effectively.*

bathroom storage

below *This elegant, shallow, dish-like basin, mounted on a tabletop, is one of the new breed of basin designs that are creating more space in small bathrooms.*

Where space is limited, fitted bathroom furniture provides the best storage, with cupboards built beneath and between the various items of sanitary ware and worktops, providing handy surfaces to hold toiletries.

Like kitchen furniture, fitted bathroom units can combine open shelves with closed cabinets, giving you quick access to regularly used items and letting linens and ceramics create their own colourful display.

If you do not want an entirely built-in look (neatness is one thing, but it can sometimes feel cold and clinical), you can create a more casual effect with free-standing furniture. Trolleys, shelf units and steel basket stands will stack 'layers' of storage one on top of another without taking up valuable floor space, and may come on castors, making it easier for you to shift them into the most practical position. Individual shelves and cabinets can then be fixed to the wall. Among the most practical are peg rails that combine a row of hooks for hanging towels, washbags, laundry bags and so on (always useful where floor space is restricted) with an integral shelf above.

Halfway between the fitted and free-standing, you can make use of areas that are crying out for built-in cupboards, while leaving the rest of the room less structured. Building a cabinet around the basin will make use of space wasted by the pedestal, and the same treatment can be given to the bath, with shallow cupboard storage built into the space behind the side panel.

BATH SURROUNDS

If there is room, it may well be worth building the bath surround out slightly – just a little will allow you to accommodate cleaning materials and spare toiletries. It should also provide a wide shelf right round the bath to add a sense of luxury – enough space for a book and a glass of wine as well as practical bath essentials. Remember, too, that the wall space on the far side of the bath, and at the head or foot if these butt up against a wall, can be fitted with shelves or hooks without obstructing the room. In a room with a high ceiling, you might also consider building the bath up on to a platform so that you can fit storage into the space beneath.

below *This elegant, shallow, dish-like basin, mounted on a tabletop, is one of the new breed of basin designs that are creating more space in small bathrooms.*

design options:

right *A mirrored door above the washbasin increases the sense of space, and conceals a deep cupboard that provides ample hidden storage for toiletries and medicines.*

WHERE TO FIND EXTRA SPACE

- Remember furniture that can play a double role is always useful where space is tight. Look for linen baskets that double as seats or bathside tables and fit tall, slim ladder radiators that provide towel racks as well as heating.

- Fit a heated towel rail beneath the basin or around the pedestal to keep towels handy and to save on precious wall space.

- Use a row of attractive baskets (the most practical are the circular woven sort, like cylindrical wastepaper baskets) to store toiletries, toilet rolls, clean flannels, cleaning materials and laundry.

- Fit the room with a deep, double-skin door with storage 'pockets' cut into the inner skin so that it can hold small items.

SMART SHELVING

Open shelves are perfect for making good use out of otherwise wasted, 'dead' space, such as narrow strips of wall behind doors. They can also be employed to create useful partitions between items of sanitary ware. For instance, you can fit a set of shelves at right angles to the wall across the foot of the bath to provide extra storage space at the same time as creating a screen to hide the lavatory.

Shelves like these are perfect for storing spare towels in attractive neatly folded piles, which can nestle in a series of square baskets. Or you can use them to display a group of colourful bath oils in interestingly shaped bottles and other aesthetically pleasing toiletries.

left *This glass basin leaves a clear run of countertop storage space for toiletries and bathroom essentials. Drawers built into the deep wooden counter help to hide clutter, and a long shelf beneath holds circular woven baskets, which are perfect for storing cleaning materials and so on. A lower row of floor baskets holds clean laundry.*

room recipe:
mosaic bathoom

colours

Clean and uncluttered, this little bathroom employs all sorts of design tricks to make the space under the eaves look far lighter and more spacious than it actually is.

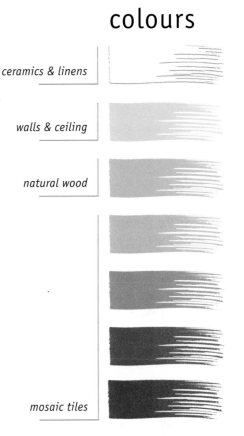

ceramics & linens

walls & ceiling

natural wood

mosaic tiles

WHY IT WORKS:

The colours are the first essential – a scheme of subtly shifting pale blues that have a receding, light-reflecting effect. This is particularly true of the plain sloping wall that continues up into the ceiling, giving the impression of a clear summer sky above you as you lie in the bath. The room's layout makes full use of this slope, with the bath positioned so that you can stand at full height at the shower end, while the other end is fitted in under the eaves.

Neat shelves incorporated into the bath surround provide plenty of space for toiletries, with additional storage supplied by a neat stacking unit that is designed to be picked up and repositioned wherever is convenient.

The skylight window, fitted in the angle of the slope, admits more light than a vertical design would allow. Keeping it free of curtains and blinds ensures that the bathroom yields the maximum benefit from it.

The triangle of the far wall has been cleverly fitted with a mirror to reflect the rest of the room and bounce light back into it, making the whole space seem bigger and lighter. The final touch is the mosaic tile design of the floor, shower wall and bath surround – a striking pattern that gives the bathroom a smart, contemporary edge. Combined with areas of plain paintwork and plain white ceramics and linens, the pattern never feels overwhelming.

KEY INGREDIENTS:

BLUE BACKGROUND
Light and space-enhancing, with a cool, refreshing quality that is perfect for bathrooms.

WHITE FITTINGS
Classic white ceramics and linens to keep the effect neutral and easy to update, and make a fresh, crisp combination with the blue.

MOSAIC TILES
Adding a luxurious, Roman-style touch and allowing you to extend the simple colour scheme into different shades, to introduce more variety of tone.

MIRRORED WALL
To reflect the light and accentuate the interesting line of the sloping ceiling.

SKYLIGHT WINDOW
Provides more privacy than a standard window, so does not need shading with curtains or blinds and can be left clear and uncluttered.

Children's rooms are self-contained worlds quite unlike anywhere else.
In contrast to adult bedrooms, they can easily become 24-hour hideouts, where children live by their own timescale, and where work, rest and play merge seamlessly into one another. Children will not think practically, so you have to do it for them – planning for durable surfaces and effective storage, while taking account of their preferences for weird colours and peer-group fads.

You could say that the best approach to furnishing these areas is to make it as easy as ABC – A being for adaptable, B for bright and C for cleanable. Adaptability is essential if the room is to cope with growing children (and possibly extra children at some stage), multiple uses, all-day activities and night-time sleepovers. Brightness is stimulating and space-making, and steers a neat path between baby pastels and teenage grunge. And cleanability is a must for all ages, however sophisticated they regard themselves. Then there are issues like safety to consider, and good lighting for bedtime reading and desk work. Plus, of course, a tabletop for homework and enough floor space to spread out toys, games and jigsaw puzzles. On top of all this, you want to create an environment where the child's imagination will flourish and develop.

With so many practicalities to tackle, it can be hard for imagination to get a look in – especially where space is limited – but creative thinking and inventive paintwork will open up other worlds and views beyond the four basic walls.

8 CHILDREN'S ROOMS

creating room to grow

Children's rooms must provide areas for private work and play, as well as safe space for sleeping. So the room must either have a separate section for each, or be flexible enough to adapt. In most homes it has to be the latter, so think laterally and get inventive.

Children's tastes and needs change much faster than those of adults. You do not want to redecorate at every stage of their development – from playing with bricks to listening to dance music – or every time they acquire a new cartoon hero or pop idol. Therefore, the trick is to stick to a background of plain colour that can be updated with accessories when a trend is outgrown or a new look called for.

It is also a good idea to get the children involved in the decorating decisions, because if they feel that the room is really theirs, they are more likely to look after it and keep it tidy. That does not mean wallpapering in the latest 'brand' pattern that will quickly outgrow its useful life: just let them help choose colours and fabrics.

left *White walls can provide a good basic background behind stimulating patterns in bolder colours, such as this lorry design, which is painted around a corner of the wall so that its yellow cab forms a side piece to the platform bed. A design like this can be painted over again at any time, making it more practical than a dominant wallpaper pattern.*

design options:

DEFINING WITH COLOUR

The usual mantra about using white to open up the space is unlikely to go down well in children's rooms. They need colour for stimulation, and although pale, space-making pastels are soothing for nurseries, once children become aware of their surroundings they will tend to be more inspired by bold, jazzy colours with a sense of fun and contemporary style. If you are letting them choose for themselves, you may need to steer them in the right direction to prevent the choice of colour resulting in an enclosed, oppressive feel. Bear in mind that yellows (being naturally lighter) and blues and greens (being receding colours) will feel less oppressive than bright reds and deep purples.

Mirrors are a great help, too, so – as long as the children are old enough to be sensible with them – you could fit cupboards with mirrored doors or use mirrored tiles to increase the space.

The best way to satisfy the demand for current crazes is to have painted walls as your base and accessorize them with peel-off borders and cutouts that can be replaced and updated. Look out, too, for luminous stick-on effects such as planets and stars to create a night sky on the ceiling, or metallic or glow-in-the-dark paint. Areas of blackboard paint will encourage creative games and writing, and magnetic paint can be used with letter and number magnets, or with fridge magnets to clip pictures to the wall. You can repaint these as often as necessary.

SAFETY CHECK

- Bunk beds are not advisable for children under six years old.
- Avoid trailing flexes and fit unused electric sockets with safety covers.
- Be careful with furniture that can trap fingers: use stoppers on doors and drawers to stop them slamming shut, and replace wooden blanket boxes with lighter baskets.
- Fit childproof window locks if window access is easy (even if it means climbing on the bed).

left *Bright green walls are both cheerful and versatile, suitable for boys and girls from toddlers to teens. The fireplace has been covered with a panel of chalkboard, providing space for the children's creative talents.*

right *This simple painted changing unit, designed with a flat top and a couple of handy storage trays, is a very practical addition to a baby's room, as it can be used as a plain chest of drawers once the child is out of nappies.*

right *Plain wooden floorboards and a subtle colour scheme make this a sophisticated but easily adaptable room for an older child. The walls have been painted in jazzy spots and graphics to match the colours of the painted furniture, plain cushions pick up the colours of the checked bedlinen, and the window is screened by a modern cut-out blind. It has enough style for any self-respecting teenager, but is easy to repaint to accommodate the next craze.*

GROUND RULES

Children's floors need to be tough, washable and – again – adaptable to different themes and colour schemes. If your children are past the messiest stage (and have reached an age where they demand a few luxuries), you could go for a comfortable carpet in a mid-tone neutral colour that will not show too many grubby marks, can be cleaned when necessary and does not restrict your decorating plans.

For younger children, cushioned vinyl or plain wood will both fit the bill, and can be covered with washable rugs and playmats for colour and comfort. It is important, however, that you add a non-slip backing so that they do not slide on polished surfaces.

The advantage of wooden floorboards is that you can repaint them as often as you want, sticking to a single all-over colour to match the furnishings, or adding patterns and games for a more inventive effect. Either use specialist floor paints for a tough, hardwearing finish, or add several coats of clear varnish to seal the colour after you have finished painting.

An alternative – if you like the idea of colour on the floor but want to keep it adaptable – is to use multicoloured carpet tiles that can be relaid in different patterns as often as you want, creating stripes, or chequers or a block of central colour contrasting with the outer border, to mimic a rug. Carpet tiles also have the practical advantage of allowing you to move worn or marked areas to a less obvious position (such as under the bed) if the flooring is beginning to look past its best.

FLEXIBLE FURNITURE

If you are thinking about adaptability, keep the furniture as simple as possible. A few specialist buys are invaluable. Beds need careful thought (see page 152) and it is useful to choose a cot that will 'grow' into a bed. And a changing unit will be essential for a small baby, but look for one with plenty of practical cupboard space so that it will still have a useful life when the baby develops beyond the nappy stage.

But over and above that, think flexibly and plan for furniture that will adapt to different uses. Instead of miniature chairs and tables, opt for squashy beanbags and basket chests that can be used for seating and storing toys when the child is older, too. Modular furniture that can be rearranged into different layouts is always an advantage, and anything on wheels is useful: attach add-on castors to furniture that does not come with its own.

This is also the place to make use of unwanted furniture from other rooms, as well as jazzed-up junk-shop or flea-market finds. When you are ruthlessly pruning pieces from the living room or your own bedroom in accordance with the clutter-control principles that you should have come to grips with, keep a lookout for any useful, adaptable cupboards and chests that can be transformed with a coat of bright (and washable) paint. Again, you can change the colour as often as you like.

ACCESSORY ACCENTS

Fabrics and bedlinens give children a bit more scope to indulge in their current crazes, although it is still best to avoid strongly branded products that will be out of date by next season. Look for bright colours and stimulating patterns – reversible if possible to provide extra variety in a single duvet cover or pillowcase.

Mixed textures make children's furnishings more fun, and help to stimulate younger children's imagination, so try to incorporate different fabrics such as furs, felt, velvet and wool. For older children, introduce intriguing accessories such as lava lamps to bridge the gap between child and adult – they will enjoy the combination of 'fun' and 'vaguely scientific', and these items also create a very soothing effect to help them sleep.

above *A combination of smart storage ideas helps control clutter. A high shelf holds books and toys, clothes are stored in a chest with colour-coded handles, and floor crates can be pushed under the bed.*

VERSATILE THEMES

Avoid blue-for-a-boy and pink-for-a-girl colour schemes that will limit your furnishing ideas and make it much more difficult to arrange for room swaps and sharing at a later stage. The same goes for gender-specific patterns such as flowers and footballers: you are better off with generic designs such as checks, stripes, spots and plains.

shared rooms

below *A Jolly Roger screen can be lowered to divide the twin beds in this pirate bedroom, giving each child his own territory behind porthole windows.*

Children need their own territory to help them establish their personality and take responsibility for their possessions. If they have to share a room, find ways to create dividing lines so that they each feel they have their own private space.

Colour-coding different areas is one of the simplest solutions with room-sharing. Let each child choose their own wall colour – or, if that seems too risky, pick two distinctive colours yourself that will work together yet create a definite contrast. You could then give each child two adjacent walls in their colour, so that the corner formed by each pair becomes their own territory. Alternatively, divide the room down the middle so that the colour changes halfway across two facing walls. You can have decorative fun with this border line by painting a wavy line or jagged zigzags so that the two colours fit together like jigsaw pieces instead of meeting as two flat edges.

Provide different styles of bedlinen to maintain the division (where possible, look for duvet designs that contain both colours, so that they coordinate well but provide contrasting patterns), and make sure that the floor changes colour, too. Boards can be painted – and repainted – as often as the need arises. Loose rugs (with non-slip backing) in contrasting shades will effect a quick change. Or you could create two reverse-image patterns with carpet tiles, designing a layout of, for example, blue tiles scattered across a green background on one side of the room, with green tiles against a blue background on the other.

DIVIDING LINES

For a more definite divide, furniture can be used to great effect, forming an actual partition between the two areas. Open shelf units are the most practical, because they provide useful storage for both sides of the room – for books, toys, CDs, school stuff and so on – but their open structure still lets light through, so that the room does not feel blocked off.

Look for wide-based, solid structures to make sure that they can stand securely without support, and children should be made clearly aware that they are not for climbing on.

left *Bright gingham panels create simple roller blinds that can be raised or lowered at times according to whether the children want private space or an open-plan play area. Chosen to match the bedlinen, they add to the room's cheerful colour scheme of blues, greens and yellows.*

Modular cube systems work particularly well, because you can devise a partition in exactly the design you want. Stack the cubes to different heights to build a battlement-like structure, or arrange them in an ascending slope so that the divide creates a sort of triangle – full height at one side of the room, reducing to ground level.

TRELLIS SCREENS

Where there is not enough room to spare for a chunky storage system, create a trellis screen instead. Again, this will maintain plenty of light in the room but will also provide useful hanging space and a pinboard background for displaying pictures and posters or sticking reminders in place. You can use standard garden trellis, either

fixing it in place as a permanent divide, or joining two or three sections together with hinges so that they form a free-standing zigzag screen that can be moved into different positions or folded away when not needed.

TEMPORARY PARTITIONS

Children are very capricious, and the clamouring for a partition could easily change to demands for a return to the open-plan room, so a flexible screen that can be supplied and removed again at short notice is a sensible idea. If you are short of floor-standing space, you could achieve a screen effect by fixing a row of ceiling-hung blinds to form a removable fabric divider that can be lowered or raised in a few seconds.

INDIVIDUAL STYLE

To emphasize the idea that each child has its own separate territory in their shared evironment, make sure that both sides of the room have plenty of display space to allow them to get creative in their own individual way. Fix pinboards to the walls to display pictures and poems, and include areas of magnetic paint (brilliant for attaching things without the need for drawing pins or sticky pads) and blackboard paint, so that they can use coloured chalks to scribble on the walls to their heart's content.

sleeping spaces

For children, the bed represents more than just a place to sleep: it is a refuge and a play area, the battleground for fantasy armies and field of dreams for a thousand imaginary games.

Adults are calculated to spend about one-third of their lives in bed, but for small children with early bedtimes, and older children with an in-built reluctance to get up in the mornings, that figure can be nearer half, so it is important to get the bed right.

ADDED DIMENSIONS

There is no point in holding out vain hope that children can be persuaded to part with unused games and toys, so the usual rules of clutter control have to be relaxed a little when it comes to planning a child's domain. It is therefore worth looking for a bed that incorporates or allows for some form of storage. At its most basic, this could simply be a frame that stands clear of the floor so that there is space to push boxes and crates underneath.

Alternatively, choose a bed with storage drawers and cupboards built into the base. It could be a classic divan type or, more imaginatively, one of the play beds or 'cabin' beds designed along bunk principles, with the mattress built up on to a platform reached by a ladder, and the lower level providing cupboards, shelves, desk space or even a full-scale playhouse underneath the bed, with doors and windows cut into the frame. You could always create a play area or private den in the space under a simple platform bed by hanging colourful curtains that can simply be drawn across.

FANTASY BEDS

Children will devise their own games around the structure, however basic it is (hence the enduring popularity of the cupboard under the stairs, and the tent improvised from blankets and a clothes horse), but if you want to give their imagination a prompt, you can find beds designed as boats,

design options:

- If you cannot envisage having space to store a cot once the child has outgrown it, you could opt for one with removable sides that converts into a proper bed, so that he or she can carry on sleeping in the same place. The most elegant are designed like French *lit bateaux*, and can even be used with cushions along the back as a sofa or daybed when the child reaches teenage years.
- Bunk beds make good use of vertical space, but standard sizes are often wider and longer than they need to be. For very small rooms, you might want to consider commissioning a reliable carpenter to build tailor-made bunks that fit your space.
- Headboards take up unnecessary room but can provide extra colour and stimulation for children. As a space-saving alternative, create your own by painting a headboard-sized panel on to the wall in your own design. Or fix a piece of corkboard to the wall and cover it with fabric, creating a few deep pockets to hold things like books, teddies, torches and other bedtime essentials.

opposite *The chunky steel-framed bunk beds provide double the sleeping space in this bedroom. The far wall is painted to recreate a maritime scene and the porthole-effect painting above the top bunk makes the room feel as if you might be on a ship.*

right *This neat bed has been built into a wood-panelled housing so that it feels safe and enclosed. The prevailing blue colour scheme of the walls and bedlinen is restful for sleep, but the cheerful yellow warms up the interior of the cabin space.*

castles, buses and spaceships. It may seem indulgent, but it is probably worthwhile if it provides a complete play centre in one piece of furniture and keeps the rest of the house clear of toys and chaos.

BUNK BEDS

Full-scale bunk beds with double-decker sleeping spaces are always a favourite with children, so exploit their enthusiasm: bunks are a godsend when two children need to share a single room or their friends need to be accommodated overnight. The frames can be made of traditional wood (which can be painted if you want to introduce extra colour in the room) or contemporary steel, which is suitably hi-tech if the bedroom has a space-age theme. Some of

the most convenient designs are made with a lower-level sofabed with a deep padded cushion along the back, so that it provides cosy seating during the daytime or when not needed as a conventional bed.

Make sure, if you do end up with a high-level bed of some sort, that you make the most of the room's height by fitting high-level shelving alongside it to match. A set of slimline shelves next to the upper mattress will provide a useful bedside bookcase as well as a surface for an alarm clock or radio.

Lamps should be clipped on to the bedframe for increased stability rather than free-standing on a high shelf, so that there is no risk of either trailing flexes or hot bulbs being knocked over on to the bedclothes.

work and play

below *This colourful teepee structure makes the bed a cosy sleeping space at night and turns the bedroom into an imaginative play area during the day.*

Work and play are starting to overlap as computers have become central to both education and entertainment. But traditional play areas and accessories are needed to encourage creative thinking and keep homework organized.

below *This colourful teepee structure makes the bed a cosy sleeping space at night and turns the bedroom into an imaginative play area during the day.*

DESK SPACE

This needs to be comfortable and well lit. Look for a worktop that can be adjusted for height so that it will 'grow' with the child and adapt from a painting table to a computer desk as he or she gets older. If there is not enough space for a permanent desk, fit a hinged wooden flap that will lie flat against the wall when not required. This can be supported either by an arm or bracket that swings out from the wall, or by sturdy ropes or chains attached to the wall above and through hooks or holes in the outer corners of the desk.

Make sure there is a good directional lamp in place so that they do not attempt to work by a gloomy overhead bulb and glare from the computer screen is minimized. If there is not enough room for it to stand on the desk, look for a jointed lamp that can be clipped to the side or on to a nearby shelf or mantelpiece. And devise some sort of noticeboard so that they have a designated place to stick messages, reminders, school timetables, invitations and so on. This could be an area of blackboard paint (used with coloured chalks) or magnetic paint (for notes to be clipped in place with fridge magnets). Instead, you could create a pinboard from a panel of cork – either left plain and used with map or drawing pins or covered with fabric and fronted with a latticework of ribbon that cards and notes can be slotted beneath.

If you are building a bespoke flap-down tabletop, the memo board can be fitted on the wall behind it so that it creates a back for the desk when folded down. Alternatively, fix it to the underside of the flap so that it is flat against the wall while the desk is not in use.

PLAY AREAS

Children – like cats – are irresistibly tempted by small cosy spaces that they can make their own, which is why beds with built-in play space beneath them are such a brilliant idea.

right *This study area has been created under the eaves to make good use of a long, narrow attic bedroom. There is plenty of natural light from windows on both sides of the sloping ceiling, as well as a spotlight set into the beam above. Bright yellow is cheerful and stimulating, and practical boxes provide storage for homework and projects.*

Most standard-sized, let alone compact, bedrooms will not offer sufficient space for a full-sized playhouse, but you may be able to box off an area – like a large cupboard – if, for instance, you have an attic room with sloping ceilings. This will make good use of a low corner that is too cramped to house items of furniture. Cut a window in the side as well as the door, and you have created an instant camp.

If there is not enough space to spare for a permanent structure like this, make use of the ideas suggested for shared rooms (see page 150) by employing screens and blinds to create temporary playhouses. Hinged screens made from garden trellis, or from painted panels of wood, or fabric stretched over a wooden frame, can be neatly folded flat against the wall and out of the way when not in use, while blinds can be hung from the ceiling to form fabric walls. Position two or three of these against an existing wall or corner and you have an instant tent. Look for brightly coloured blinds, or opt for plain cotton and paint them with your own design to represent a castle, or shop or whatever craze is currently in favour.

FLOOR FUN

Use the floor to provide imaginative play ideas, too. Paint giant chequers or spots on to the floorboards for instant games of hopscotch and Twister, and add washable playmats designed as farmyards, railways or street layouts so that the children are inspired to create their own games.

Find slots under beds and chests for things like toy forts and farmyards to avoid them being folded up and boxed away every time they are used. Add plenty of labelled crates and draw-string bags for sets of bricks, construction kits and so on (see page 156 for more storage ideas).

DESK ESSENTIALS

Provide plenty of containers to hold desk essentials: kitchen cutlery trays are perfect for pencils, crayons, paperclips and so on. Add a memo board or an area of chalkboard or magnetic paint so that children have a place for messages, reminders, school timetables and so on.

clever storage

Good storage is key to making small bedrooms work, and the key to kids' storage is to make it fun, so that they will actually consider using it. Exploit every possible corner and encourage your children to organize their possessions by keeping clothes, school things and play things separate.

Low-level storage is the most practical for young children, which they can easily reach and put things away for themselves. Baskets and crates that will slide under a bed can also be stacked against a wall so that they do not take up so much floor space. Picnic hampers and laundry baskets make good toy boxes as the lids are light and will not trap small fingers. Plastic crates that fit together for neat stacking will create a colourful display rather like a tower of building blocks, or you can find frames to hold them. The most useful of these come on wheels to form a sort of movable trolley; choose semi-transparent boxes so that you can see what is inside.

CUBE SYSTEMS

Cube storage is ideal, as the arrangement can be changed as children grow, starting with a single row of units along the wall to provide low-level cupboards or open slots with a deep shelf or seat on top, and then building them up to higher levels as the child gets older and wants space for books, CDs, music systems and so on. You can also slot individual containers, such as shoe boxes and filing crates, into the cubes to hold smaller items.

It is worth painting the cubes to make them more interesting. Colour is important if you want the idea of storage to appeal to messy children: basic wardrobes and chests of drawers can be painted in harlequin shades to brighten them up, each drawer a different colour, or doors and handles contrasting with the main structure.

FABRIC COVERS

If you despair of children being able to keep open shelves tidy, you can easily turn them into cupboards by fitting curtains or blinds to cover them.

above *This spacious cupboard has been fitted with extra storage to hold clothes and accessories – including a hanging shoe rack.*

design options:

Fabric covers are simple to make and are an economical and space-saving alternative to solid woodwork. You could also opt for canvas or plastic clothes hangers rather than full-scale wardrobes; these are much less bulky and provide plenty of adaptable storage to keep children organized. Bear in mind that children do not in general need as much hanging clothes space as adults (most clothes can be folded and laid flat) and what hanging space they do need will be shorter.

Fix storage tubes (open cylinders of cardboard or perspex) to the walls to hold school artwork and posters without crushing or folding them. Neatest of all, fix up a length of wall-mounted trellis to which you can attach as many hooks as you want without damaging the surface behind. Do not forget overhead space. Lengths of webbing (like fishing net) and trellis panels can be suspended from the ceiling to provide extra storage, especially for soft toys that will not hurt themselves or anyone else if they fall.

above *Painted pegrails fixed to the wall provide handy hanging space for toys, clothes and shoe bags. Keep a stock of drawstring bags that can be used to hold socks, other crush-proof clothes and laundry, as well as shoes.*

above right *Colourful crates and boxes are always useful. Stack them against the wall or push them under beds and on top of wardrobes to tidy bedroom clutter out of the way and store clothes and games not currently in use.*

HANGING STORAGE

Anything that keeps the floor clear is useful, so fix plenty of hooks and pegs for hanging storage. Drawstring bags hung from these can be used to store toys, clothes, shoes and laundry, with plastic beach buckets holding smaller items – farm animals, magnetic numbers and letters, crayons and so on.

CREATIVE CUPBOARDS

Use your creative talents to devise colours, effects and trompe l'oeil façades that incorporate storage into the overall style of the room, so that the cupboards become part of the decoration and open up imaginative new worlds rather than seeming a waste of good play space.

- Paint a lighthouse on to a tall cupboard to create the background for a seaside-style room.
- Do the same with a helter-skelter to conjure up a fairground setting.
- Turn a little girl's cupboard into a doll's house façade. You could even divide up the shelves inside so that they make different 'rooms'.
- Fit tongue-and-groove panelled doors across alcoves to turn them into cupboards, with rope pull handles for a nautical, beach-house effect.
- Paint a narrow cupboard door in bright stripes reminiscent of a Punch and Judy theatre, or hang a panel of striped fabric for an even more authentic effect.
- Create a jousting-tent cupboard, with a painted pelmet fixed over an alcove to form the turret top, and a length of striped fabric that can be rolled up like a blind for access to the shelves behind.
- Paint a cupboard in alternating blocks of colour for a harlequin pattern. Mark out your design in pencil first, and use masking tape to give each square a neat edge, peeling the tape off after the paint is dry and the pattern complete.

colours

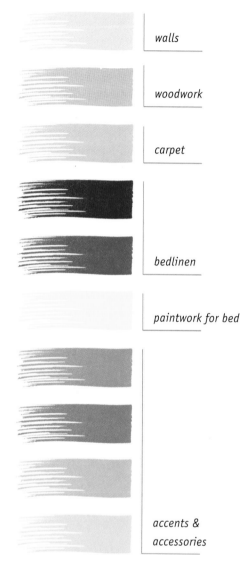

walls

woodwork

carpet

bedlinen

paintwork for bed

accents & accessories

room recipe:
attic hideaway

The key to this room is its clever bed design, which is high enough to allow for ample drawers and cupboards to be built in underneath the mattress, without using up all the available wall space.

WHY IT WORKS:

Neat under-bed storage like this is perfect for clothes and spare bedlinen, as well as all the toys and extra clutter that tends to accumulate in children's rooms. The colour contributes to the effect, too, with the storage fronts painted bright yellow to contrast with the room's blue paintwork. The whole effect is fresh and simple, the pale blue walls providing plenty of space and light reflection and the yellow adding a touch of cheerful sunshine.

The basic floor is plain wooden boards – easy to keep clean and to update when required. The simple blue rug, edged with a darker linen border, adds temporary colour and comfort. There is also plenty of pattern offered by the mixed bedlinens, which combine geometric squares and stripes with bold coloured spots: nothing too brand-specific that might quickly be outgrown, but bright and stimulating to keep a child interested in its surroundings.

Head room may not be so important in a child's room, but this layout makes the most of the limited space anyway, by tucking in the bed under the sloping ceiling and positioning the homework area opposite the window so that the desk gets plenty of light. The desk is painted to match the bed to prevent it from feeling too much like work, and the chair can be folded away and neatly stowed in the deep window recess when not in use.

KEY INGREDIENTS:

STORAGE BED
Raised on a platform to provide plenty of storage underneath it, and painted a bright colour to make the idea of storage more fun.

PALE BLUE WALLS
This makes the most of the attic light without dominating the room too much – a good colour to take as the starting point for a practical furnishing scheme.

STIMULATING PATTERNS
Spots, stripes and geometric shapes are scattered across the bedlinen in bright contrasting colours.

PRACTICAL FLOORING
Neat laminate boards beneath a soft, colourful rug. The rug can be washed or replaced when necessary and the boards are hardwearing enough to withstand rough treatment.

WINDOW RECESS
A natural feature is put to hard-working use both as a window seat and a handy storage area for toys and games.

Studios and open-plan apartments have an unstructured, liberating feel which creates a relaxed atmosphere the moment you enter. There are no walls to block the light or restrict the view, and no doorways limiting movement to narrow access points. But you have your work cut out for you in finding areas to accommodate all your everyday activities.

So where there is plenty of overhead space, it is worth taking full advantage of this to create a second, mezzanine floor – an additional level halfway between the two existing floors. This instantly gives the room an extra dimension and suggests all sorts of new possibilities for how you are going to live in it. Add a flight of stairs to a single-floor apartment and you instantly turn it into a house, opening up its space and angles, creating variety and interest that do not usually exist on a single flat level. Rather like a garden that has been stepped to create separate terraces, a split-level room presents the visitor with a richer, more complete picture, and provides focal points beyond the immediate space. It helps to demarcate different areas, too, by keeping sleeping or study space distinct from the living space while maintaining the overall open-plan feel.

Your mezzanine level could be a single platform across one end of the room, or an L-shape or horseshoe design with galleries running back along one or both side walls. The upper level will have interesting views over the main space, and the height also gives it its own sense of privacy because it cannot be overlooked.

9 SPLIT-LEVEL LIVING

mapping the space

When confronted with a single-space living area, establish what you need in order to make the best use of it. There are certain key activities – cooking, bathing and sleeping – but beyond that, the space is yours. How you live in it is up to you.

Getting to know your space and how you are likely to use it is always important, but when you only have one room to play with – and all of it visible from the moment you walk through the front door – it is essential. The disadvantage is that you cannot really make any decorative decisions for a while because there is no one area that can be isolated from the rest: the whole space needs to work as a single entity, which can feel a daunting prospect and an unwieldy project to conjure with. But the advantage of a single space is that, because you are in all of it all of the time, you will find it much easier to try out different arrangements and see instantly what effect they have.

In a multi-room house, you can only get a feel for one room at a time, gradually building up a jigsaw of how you want to live in it, but one-room living gives you the whole picture in one go. Try a particular area as a sitting room and you will see what space that leaves you for eating, sleeping and so on. Try another for sleeping, and you may realize that it is taking up valuable window space that would be much more effectively used as a daytime living area.

UPSTAIRS, DOWNSTAIRS

The immediate assumption about galleries and mezzanine floors is that they will provide sleeping space – yet another reflection of the deep-rooted tradition of always going upstairs to bed. But if the ceiling is high enough to allow you to stand upright, there is no reason why this upper level could not be put to equally good use as a study, sitting space, dining area or even a kitchen, according to your requirements.

You really need an original ceiling height of at least 4.5m (15ft), and preferably 5m (16ft), if you are planning to add a full-height mezzanine, while purpose-built loft-style mezzanines are often higher, with the whole space acting more like a normal two-storey house but the upper floor cut back to create an open gallery.

above *This split-level apartment makes full use of its vertical space by accentuating the upright lines of the stair column and the gallery rail. A spiral staircase provides access to yet another level, without taking up any valuable floor space.*

design options:

TRICKS OF THE LIGHT

- Light is one of the key considerations when deciding how to divide up the space, and it depends largely on the positioning of the windows. In the case of a split-level building, this will vary according to whether the room was specifically designed on two levels or has been adapted by the addition of an upper gallery in a high-ceilinged room.

- If the room was originally designed as a single space, the upper floor is more than likely to be above the level of the windows, in which instance it will be naturally darker and a sensible place to site your sleeping area.

- If the room was originally on two levels, however, there will probably be plenty of light on the upper floor either from purpose-built windows or skylights. It would, therefore, be a shame to waste this by saving the space for night-time use when you could be taking advantage of it during the daytime.

AUTHENTIC MATERIALS

Use natural materials such as wood, brick and stone to emphasize the architecture of the space, accent its lines and, in the case of warehouse conversions, reflect the building's original use. It is always best to incorporate any structural pillars and columns as part of your overall design rather than trying to disguise them. Use staircases and handrails as architectural features, choosing shapes and materials with care in order to create dramatic visual effects.

colour and style

below *Arched windows provide light for upper and lower levels in this warehouse conversion. Fitting the upper gallery with panels of glass increases the light flow.*

In a split-level space, try to keep the whole area as light as possible, and use a single, unifying colour for the main wall and ceiling surfaces.

Even if the gallery will be used as a sleeping or eating area, so that it could in theory take the darker, more enclosing colours suitable for bedrooms and dining rooms, bear in mind that, in an open-plan room like this, how you treat one part of it will affect the rest of the space, too. Dark, moody colours overhead will appear to lower the ceiling instead of maintaining the sense of height that you need for a modern, space-making setting.

If you want to add stronger colours, use them on surfaces that are recessed behind the mezzanine parapet. By painting cupboard doors or far walls on the upper level in a bright colour, for instance, you will provide interest and focal points from the floor below without overwhelming a predominantly neutral scheme.

FOLLOWING THE ARCHITECTURE

Light, neutral colours are the most effective at opening up a space like this, but you can adapt a neutral background to establish different effects by adding other materials and surfaces to suit the building's architecture. The high ceilings that allow for galleries and mezzanines tend to be found either in modern industrial-style buildings such as warehouses and loft conversions or in classically proportioned older buildings.

MODERN SPACES

In contemporary settings, a combination of white-painted walls with areas of exposed brickwork and fittings in natural wood, steel and glass will create an appropriately industrial look and conjure up an instant sense of loft living. Staircases can be designed with wooden treads fitted into steel sides and with steel handrails. Gallery balustrades can be in wood, steel, tensioned wire or – at a cost – toughened glass, for a really sleek, light-enhancing finish.

OLDER BUILDINGS

Older buildings are likely to have traditional features such as ornate plasterwork and deep sash windows, which need to be accommodated

by any gallery level you add. Modern mezzanine fittings such as glass and steel can create an interesting contrast in a setting like this, but you may find the clash of old and new materials visually uncomfortable.

Judge the individual room according to its shape and architectural line, and trust your instincts. White-painted wood for the staircase and balustrading will keep the effect light and contemporary but have a mellower feel than glass and steel. You could leave the wood unpainted, but be careful that it does not look dark and gloomy, especially on the upper level.

To match the practical nature of the gallery with the natural elegance of the room, aim for a simplicity reminiscent of a traditional chapel or schoolroom, where whitewashed walls are restful and understated despite the imposing high ceilings and windows.

Make use of any high ceiling beams, supports, struts and so on that are visible up in the roof space to create architectural drama and contrast against the light background. Whether these are steel, painted or plain wood, they will help to accentuate the shape of room without intruding too much on it.

design options:

OCEAN-GOING STYLE

- The idea of an upper gallery with a balustrade overlooking the main room has a distinctly nautical look to it, rather like the upper deck of an ocean liner. This is especially the case where steel supports or reinforced joists are visible, and staircases are flanked by functional steel handrails.
- To combine the practical feel of the structure with a sense of the luxury of classic 1930s liners, lay sleek wood floors and add streamlined Art Deco-style furniture such as curved-back tub chairs and kitchen countertops cut in a sweeping curve.

left *A simple wooden staircase leads to a gallery sleeping area beneath a sloping roof. White paintwork against the deep blue walls accents the interesting architectural lines.*

flexible furnishings

below *A freestanding unit provides storage on the reverse side, while also acting as an informal partition, screening off the far side of the room.*

The beauty of open-plan living is its flexibility. The balance of floor space to overhead space makes it comparable to a stage set, and that gives you the most tremendous potential to use the area in different ways and for different effects.

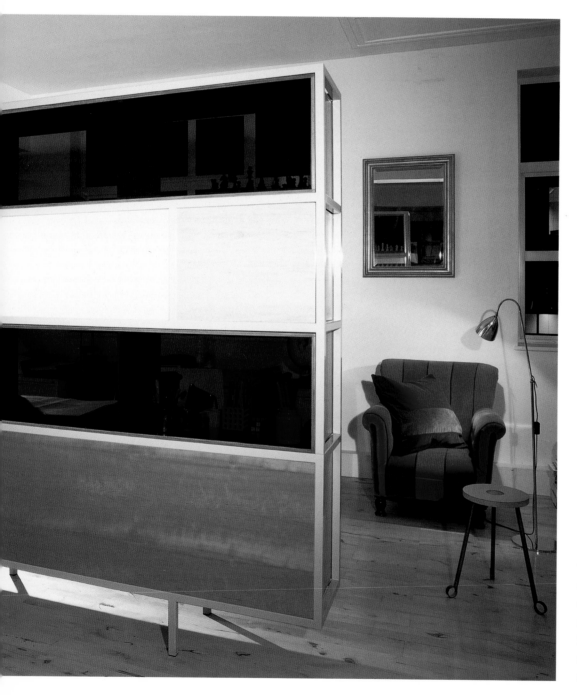

A FRESH TAKE

The positions of the kitchen and bathroom will be fixed once you have decided on them, but the rest of the space can be rearranged as often as you want, by moving the furniture, shifting screens and partitions, adjusting the lighting and redeploying areas for different activities when you feel like a change.

Change is as important in furnishing as it is in any other area of life. Seeing things from a new angle is refreshing and energizing – it revitalizes the spirit and stimulates the imagination. The simple act of moving the furniture around will give any room a new lease of life, but in an open-plan living space, the effect will be more far-reaching, letting you design yourself a whole new home. Because there are no walls dividing it into fixed areas, there are absolutely no restrictions on what you put where, just the freedom to use the space as you want.

THE THREE-DIMENSIONAL VIEW

What you will need to do, though, is make the best possible use of the floor space to avoid cluttering up the open, free-flowing feel with unnecessary furniture. This means fewer pieces, and neater designs, so that the space feels in proportion. Be sure to keep the idea of the stage set in mind, selecting scaled-down furniture and positioning it where it looks good from every conceivable angle. Avoid grouping decorative objects or pictures together so that they read as a cluttered whole, and leave plenty of breathing space in between them.

Because the entire space is visible at once, open-plan areas have a more three-dimensional feel to them than ordinary rooms. If you think about it, we are used to getting our first view of a room from its doorway, like an image in a photograph, but where there are no doors between the different areas, this 'flat' view is opened up into one with an increased sense of depth and perspective.

design options:

above *The wardrobe unit here acts as an internal wall between the foreground living area and the bedroom in the background. The low leather armchair suits the modern style of the space, and skylight windows provide the living area with plenty of natural sunlight.*

LIGHT AND SLEEK SURFACES

Try to incorporate cool, light-reflective surfaces that will blend into the background rather than making a dramatic visual statement or focal point. Look for furniture designed in pale wood, slimline steel, glass and perspex.

FURNITURE DESIGN

The key to keeping your furniture neat is to make sure it can lay claim to at least one of the following benefits:

● **Clean, streamlined design** Certain shapes create the feeling of space more than others. Circular or oval tables have no protruding corners and will seat more people in a smaller area. Long, thin dining tables will seat as many people as shorter, wider ones and will not obstruct the room so much. Chairs and sofas with low, square-cut arms are neater than squashy, scroll-armed designs.

● **Folding or stacking ability** Besides chairs, look for tables that will fold away: perhaps trestle and wallpapering tables that will stand against a wall when not in use.

● **Dual function** Avoid furniture that is designed for a specific room when it could fulfil a more general need. For example, do not opt for dressing tables that limit themselves to bedroom use but choose chests of drawers or blanket boxes that could be used anywhere; look for low tables that would work just as well beside the bed or in the sitting area; steel-topped tables that will double as kitchen worktops and dining tables; upright chairs that could be used for dining, breakfast or out in the garden; stools and cubes that will switch from chairs to tables, depending on which you need at the time; trunks and chests providing storage space inside and seating or table surfaces on top.

structural issues

You need to make a distinction between a wooden sleeping platform that is really just a glorified bunk bed and could be built by a reliable carpenter, and a mezzanine level designed for regular use that will require the help of a structural engineer.

A proper mezzanine will be robust, probably with a frame in steel or reinforced concrete, or in flitch beam, which comprises a thin layer of steel sandwiched between wooden beams so that the steel adds strength and the wood holds the steel rigid. If this is what you are planning, you will need to involve a structural engineer.

The gallery structure itself will need adequate support by load-bearing walls to make sure that it can take the weight of people and additional furniture. Some of the simplest designs take advantage of floor-standing support, constructed on a solid framework that provides storage underneath but not open, usable living space. These are often lower, perhaps around head-height, so that there would not be enough room to stand upright beneath the platform anyway. A full-scale mezzanine, on the other hand, can either span the width of the room with walls on both sides supporting it, or be cantilevered out with the load carried by a single wall. You may also need the support of a column or pillar underneath – you can use this to help define the space of the lower level.

You probably will not need planning permission, as you are not affecting the exterior of the house (unless you want to fit a new window as part of your mezzanine), but you will need to comply with building regulations. Take your plans to your local planning office to have them checked.

ACCESS AND SAFETY

Access to the mezzanine can be by stairs or ladder (although ladders will need to be rigid and equipped with a handrail, such as the sort designed for lofts). The steeper the stairs, the

left *This arrangement provides a sleeping platform in the unused ceiling height above the kitchen. The extra-steep stairs also create neat storage slots in the ends of their treads, to hold kitchen provisions and display items.*

more floor space you will save, so you could consider a spiral staircase (see page 67). But think about practicality, too. Ladders and steep stairs are much easier to go up than they are to come down, so if your gallery is to be a sleeping area involving access at night, you might want to opt for something less precipitous.

You will need to be especially careful if children are likely to use the space, but safety is an issue for adults, too. As a general rule, any staircase of more than four or five steps really

needs some sort of handrail – both for grip and to provide a barrier on the open side. You could find it difficult to satisfy building regulations without this, so look for solutions such as glass and tensioned wire that will meet the required specifications without spoiling your design. Also bear in mind that the height of the upper level will restrict your lighting options up here: recessing lights into the ceiling is the most space-saving solution, and will also avoid the risk of touching hot light bulbs.

opposite *A narrow, steep staircase provides access to the upper-level sleeping gallery without disrupting the living space. The ironwork of the structure continues to form the gallery rail for a unified look. The kitchen is partitioned off but still linked by an open corridor.*

BUILDING REGULATIONS

If in any doubt about safety or what will satisfy building regulations, contact your local planning office for their guidance. Planning permission should not present an obstacle unless you are wanting to add extra windows. If you need extra light, consider installing skylights instead, which do not alter the roof outline and therefore should meet with official approval. Some companies make a particular design of skylight that opens out to provide an escape route in case of fire, which will also help you to satisfy building regulations.

designing for privacy

below *Deep shelves
provide book storage for
the bedroom and divide
the sleeping and living
areas. The space is
unified by white walls
and natural flooring.*

Once you have established a mezzanine level,
it is up to you how much privacy you allocate to
both floors. You can create effective visual
divisions without danger of disrupting the open-
plan feel, but you may want to screen off
sleeping or study areas to keep them quieter and
less overlooked.

On the upper level, you can achieve privacy
with glass walls (either clear or frosted) or
Japanese-style sliding doors (paper or stretched
fabric panels fitted into wooden frames to create
a light-filtering screen). If you are more worried
about privacy than noise, you could install a row
of tall plants along the gallery balustrade, to
provide an organic screen and create an
interesting view from below.

The presence of the gallery will give part
of the ground floor a lower ceiling, creating a
natural divide that you might want to accentuate.
The space beneath the mezzanine will
automatically feel more enclosed, so this could
be a good area to position a bedroom or
bathroom, and as the light is already slightly
limited, you will not be blocking it further by
adding a screen of some sort.

Sliding doors and ceiling-hung blinds will give
you the option of switching from a closed room
to an open area whenever you want. Or you
could opt for a rigid wall but one that only
screens off part of the space – perhaps to
conceal a cooking area – while leaving a wide
entrance that feels more like an open-sided room
than a doorway. If you do not want to go to the
trouble of erecting proper partition walls, you
can create the same effect with floor-standing
bookshelves, and provide some useful storage
capacity at the same time.

SCREENS AND STORAGE

Where everything else is open to view, storage
is the one thing you might prefer to keep behind
closed doors, to make sure that the space
maintains its streamlined, uncluttered feel.
If you are aiming at a completely open-plan,
unstructured room, this kind of storage will need
to be built in around the walls to keep the floor
free. Remember that you now have an extra level,
taking wall storage to new heights.

design options:

You could also add storage beneath the platform, especially if it is a low-level gallery that can be boxed off underneath to provide deep, roomy cupboards. The upper level, being less immediately visible, could take open bookshelves without creating a cluttered impression. If your mezzanine has a narrow side gallery, you could use this to line the upper wall with bookshelves to give a library effect when viewed from below.

If, however, you want to create some sort of divide between different areas, it is worth planning your storage at the same time, simply because they are so often provided by the same furniture. Shelf units will become practical dividers if carefully positioned. Even a low one will be enough to demarcate between sitting and study space, for instance.

Free-standing screens create extra on-the-spot wall space that can also be used for display (in other words, storage for pictures).

PORTABLE STORAGE

If the idea of too much built-in storage undermines your concept of an open-plan room that needs to stay as flexible as possible, take advantage of the many free-standing cupboards, chests and shelf units that now come on wheels, so that you can move them into new positions when needed (and out of the way when not). These will keep your layout as flexible as you want.

- Kitchen-style trolleys, incorporating shelves and drawers, can be just as useful in a study area.
- Bedrooms can be equipped with shop-style hanging rails so that even your wardrobe feels portable.

above *A partition wall half-divides the kitchen from the dining room, demarcating the two areas without isolating them completely. Sleek furniture designs in pale wood and reflective chrome are neat and space-saving.*

right *High windows provide this upper gallery with plenty of light, making it a perfect place for a study area. A line of plants behind the rail creates a living screen to give the office space a little more privacy.*

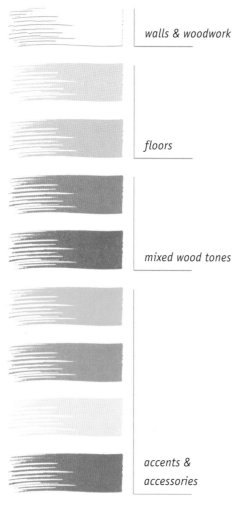

walls & woodwork

floors

mixed wood tones

accents & accessories

room recipe:
galleried living

This is the perfect split-level arrangement. The lower level provides plenty of living, eating and cooking space for daytime use, while the low-ceilinged gallery above has just enough room for desk work, sitting and sleeping.

WHY IT WORKS:

Nothing is wasted in this design; the height of the gallery has been positioned to balance the shape of the space, squaring off the lower room by lowering a ceiling that would have looked unnaturally high for its width.

Keeping the walls and woodwork white unifies the overall space and reflects plenty of light, and the staircase is narrow enough not to intrude into the downstairs room. Painting the edges of the treads white makes them look even narrower, as the eye reads the central plain wood section rather than the full stair width.

Downstairs, the kitchen has been tucked out of the way at the far end of the room. Mellow wooden cabinets suit their situation as part of the living area, but reflective ceramic tiles add to the light-enhancing effect of the chrome appliances. A glass-topped table and streamlined, stackable chairs are as space-saving as dining furniture can be, keeping the floor area relatively clear and leaving a path for access to the stairs and front door.

The changing floor coverings – from tiles to carpet to wooden stairs – demarcate these different areas effectively without breaking up the overall unity of the space. Upstairs, the sofa folds out into a bed at night, and the work desk becomes a bedside table. Wall lights and a jointed, directional table lamp avoid the need for conventional ceiling lights.

KEY INGREDIENTS:

LIGHT COLOURS
Neutral walls, pale wood chairs and kitchen cabinets, and a soft mossy carpet are accented by surfaces in glass and chrome.

SPACE-SAVING FURNITURE
A glass-topped table does not block out the light, and stacking slim-legged chairs can be stored out of the way when not in use.

UPSTAIRS SLEEPING SPACE
An upper level is used for sitting and sleeping (where the ceiling does not need to be full height) to make the most of the vertical space.

NARROW STAIRCASE
This is designed with white-painted edges so that it looks even narrower than it is, and cuts no more than a slim slice off the main room.

BRIGHT ACCESSORIES
Touches of colour bring the whole setting to life by providing an effective contrast with the neutral background.

When you have squeezed all the space you can out of your home, the only remaining option is to expand outwards or upwards, pushing the boundaries to create new rooms beyond the existing framework.

The direction you move in depends partly on the structure of the building and partly on what you plan to use the new room for. If you can gain entry to the roof, converting the loft with proper access, windows and furnishings can give you a new bedroom, bathroom or office area. If you have a garden, you could build out into it, either creating an extra room in the form of a conservatory or extension, or by furnishing a veranda or decking area to create an outdoor room for use in the summer months.

One of the best things about moving the boundaries of your home is that the new space you acquire is almost always lighter than any of your existing rooms, so you get a real sense of opening up your house and extending your living space into the outside world. Another advantage is that breaking the mould like this frees up the way you look at your space. So a glass extension need not be kept for summer and hot-house plants – capitalize on the light and use it as a study or a living room.

Take that concept a stage further and you can overturn the conventional assumptions about home layout and see new potential for making the most of it.

10 EXTENDING YOUR SPACE

lofts and attics

Adding an extra floor on to your home has the feel of a miracle about it. You do not need to move house, you can keep the rest of the layout exactly as it is and you gain up to 40 per cent more usable space in one fell swoop.

Expanding through the roof may simply mean devising some sort of easy access to your attic, putting down a floor that you can walk on safely and kitting it out with practical storage for spare furniture and old school reports. Fitted with lighting, the same sort of arrangement could become a playroom or occasional workroom if you are prepared to put up with colder temperatures than the rest of the house.

But with proper heating, insulation, plumbing, furnishings and soundproofing, you can turn the space into anything from a home office or a master bedroom-and-bathroom suite to a completely self-contained flat. Roof space is perfect for offices and adult bedrooms – or as a personal flat if you want to rent out lower rooms – because it is up above the everyday noise of the house and sound tends to travel downwards.

left *Sliding glass doors pull back to link this dining room extension to the top-floor kitchen, providing a completely glazed area that gets natural light from all directions. The sense of a single space is reinforced by the smart wooden flooring.*

design options:

right *This attic has been converted into a bedroom, with the simple sleeping space fitted under the sloping ceiling where there is less standing room. The exposed-brick wall and industrial-style handrail maintain the functional converted-warehouse feel of the building.*

PLANNING PERMISSION

- Check for potential planning permission problems before you start commissioning architects or builders. As long as all you are doing is levelling out the existing slope of the roof into a flat surface (rather than building up from the existing ridge height), you may not have much difficulty. The only obstacles will be if you live in a conservation area, or if the house is listed for architectural interest or you want to fit dormer windows in the new roof.
- Dormers may be turned down if they overlook a road or a neighbour's house, or if they change the line of the roof. You can usually gauge what is possible from looking at other houses in your street to see which projects have been granted planning approval. Whatever you are planning, check with the authorities early on to avoid disappointment and expense.

PRACTICAL PLANNING

The first thing to establish is whether your roof is suitable for a full-scale extension. The house really needs a pitched roof if it is going to provide enough usable space for a proper, regularly used room. As a general guide, living areas should have a height of at least 2.3m (7ft 8in) from the top of the existing ceiling joists (the level that will be the floor of the new room) to the apex under the ridge of the new roof. You can sometimes get away with a lower height in kitchens, bathrooms, playrooms, corridors and storage spaces, but building regulations in your area may enforce these official guidelines.

You will also need to make sure that you end up with a minimum wall height of 1.5m (5ft) where the slope of the room meets the wall of the building. Ridge roofs, which have flat gable end walls, are easier to convert than hipped roofs, where the ends slope as well so there are four slanting surfaces to deal with.

You will also need to plan for access to your new floor. You may be able to extend the existing stairs into an extra flight from the top landing, but it is more likely that you will have to create a steeper route, such as a vertical-drop spiral staircase or a specially designed flight (sometimes called an 'alternator' staircase) with extra-steep treads so that it takes up less room than a standard flight.

LETTING IN THE LIGHT

To make the space as light as possible, try to aim for a window area equivalent to at least 10 per cent of your floor space. Windows or French doors can provide daylight (with a railing or balcony) in gable ends, and by dormers or skylights installed in the roof pitch itself. Dormers will increase your views and headroom, but may be prohibited by planning regulations.

Skylights are an easier option because they follow the line of the roof. They are also cheaper to fit because they do not need scaffolding (installation can be can be done from inside) and they let in 50 per cent more light than vertical windows, but you will need tinted glass or good blinds to shade them during the day.

PALE PALETTE

Assuming this is going to be at least partly a daytime room, stick to pale colours and neutral flooring to enhance the sense of light and space

right *Bright, white walls and natural flooring create a light, spacious bedroom under the eaves. Practical chests, which are in pale wood to match the colour scheme, are fitted under the lowest part of the ceiling to provide plenty of storage without using up valuable floor space.*

opposite *Attic rooms make good bedrooms as you will be up above the noise of the rest of the house. Let the building's architecture guide your decisions when extending your home, and make sure you have your plans checked so that they comply with building regulations.*

in your loft conversion. You could go for deeper colours if you want it to be a womb-like bedtime retreat, but it is a terrible waste of the top-floor sunlight that a well-designed loft will capture during the day.

Walls in white, cream or pale pastels will be well complemented by neutral carpet, natural matting or a plain wood floor. Natural wood will look sleek and smart, or you could go for simple white-painted boards to maximize the light and add a beach-house or artist's studio look. Even if you opt for a soft floor, make sure you fit top-

quality sound-proofing beneath it to reduce noise levels on the floors below – you will really notice it if you fail to do this.

EXPLOITING STORAGE SPACE

The whole point of converting your loft is to give you more space, so plan your layout to make the best possible use of it. Have as much built-in storage as possible to keep the floor area clear of clutter and bulky furniture. Design your cupboards and shelves around the slope of the ceilings, so that you have full-height space for

design options:

TIPS FOR LOFT CONVERSIONS

- Plan for and lighting, heating, insulation, power points, telephone connections, plumbing and safety requirements from the outset. Make sure you that include enough power points to supply lamps, tools, games, computers and other equipment you want to use.

- If you are planning to install a bathroom in your loft conversion, you should bear in mind that the cold water storage tank will need to be as high as possible to pressurize the taps. For a power shower, you need at least 1.5m (5ft) between the base of the tank and the shower head (otherwise you should consider installing an electric pump).

- Building regulations may require at least one window in case of fire and adequate staircase access and fire doors with self-closing mechanisms. Check the building regulations with your local planning office.

- You will have to consider soundproofing any walls adjoining your neighbours' houses in order to keep disturbance levels right down, and in some areas building regulations will stipulate that you must do so.

- Contact your planning department for advice before you start, then find a structural engineer who can turn your ideas into a structurally safe plan. Makes friends with your local building control surveyor and get him to check that the plans meet building regulations.

items that need it, such as hanging coats and dresses, with smaller items fitted into the corner of the slope. Build low cupboards or deep pull-out drawers right into the eaves: the ceiling height is lowest here and the space would otherwise be wasted.

FINISHING TOUCHES

Restrict window dressing to simple blinds or linen panels to shade the light without obstructing the space, and fit recessed spotlights or wall uplighters rather than hanging pendants, which will get in the way where ceilings are low. Make use of interesting radiator shapes, such as spirals and ladders, to create designer effects where there is little wall space. If you are fitting a loft bathroom, look for back-to-the-wall or wall-hung fittings to save space and hide messy pipework.

WORK IN PROGRESS

Most loft conversions are tackled from a scaffolding frame, otherwise you have to break through the roof from the inside, which means that existing upper rooms are out of action while the work is going on, and lower rooms are exposed to additional cold and dirt. Either way, be prepared for mess and upheaval throughout the work. Doors should be taped up to prevent dust filtering down the house and getting into other rooms.

conservatories and glass extensions

If you have not got access to the roof of the building, you may be able to build outwards with a conservatory, or by glazing in a gap between two buildings or across a central 'well'.

If you are thinking about a glass extension, check first about planning permission. Whether or not you need permission usually depends on the percentage increase in floor space you are creating. Conservatories can even be built on to upper floors – on roof terraces or stilts – although planning permission will probably be more of a problem.

INDOORS, OUTDOORS

Banish the image of the sunroom tacked on to a suburban house. The real beauty of a conservatory is its dual nature: shifting between indoor garden and outdoor room, it can open up both spaces as it captures the sun and provides shelter from the wind. Whether it is framed with wood or aluminium, the simple fact is that there is nothing to match all that glass for providing light, views and a sense of the outside world. Make sure it is heated, insulated and ventilated for all seasons and weathers, and use it to extend the boundaries of your home or to fill the gap between the arms of an L-shape.

The most important thing is to get the architectural style right. The concept of the conservatory is centuries old, so some of the most elegant designs are very traditional in form – beautifully crafted but with too much ornamental detail for a modern setting. What you need is something that looks like a logical extension of the house, and also matches the style and layout of the garden. Think of it as a room with a glass ceiling and glass walls, and you will find that simpler, less obviously 'antique' designs often create the most effective links, even if the original building itself is old.

Furnishings depend on what the room will be used for. Glass spaces make excellent dining rooms and kitchens, where you need not spend

all day if you do not want to, but can enjoy lingering on sunny days. They are also a good way of extending a sitting room, so that you still have an enclosed, cosy part, but one end feels lighter and more open.

To maximize the sense of extending your boundaries and opening up the house, aim for a style that makes the space feel like part of the building rather than as a bolt-on extra.

above This simple conservatory occupies the gap between the kitchen and the garden wall. Solid-sided, with a glass roof and glazed doors to the garden, it provides a sun-filled room for year-round use.

design options:

right *This extension, with its sloping glass roof, pushes the house out into the garden and creates a breakfast room alongside the existing kitchen. Furnishing it with classic furniture and an elegant light fitting reinforces the sense that it is a proper room, not a little-used summer suntrap.*

Treat it as a room rather than a conservatory, and avoid the cane-and-rattan furniture look that will again typecast it as a conventional sunroom.

ALL-WEATHER FLOORING

The floor needs to be durable, easy to maintain and resistant both to damp and to changes in temperature. Terracotta tiles will work well in kitchens and dining rooms, and accentuate the closeness of the garden. They are particularly appropriate and practical if you want to include plants as part of your furnishings.

Linoleum and vinyl are an alternative for kitchens. Wood looks wonderful, but you need to make sure that your conservatory is well shaded and waterproofed, as strong sunlight and damp can cause timber floors to warp and split. Carpet is probably best avoided if the room will have direct access to the garden, because mud and grass will stain it easily.

WALL CHOICES

The sides may be entirely of glass, or the lower walls may be in brick – useful if you to want to provide the room with low-level storage, which can be built against them. If the glazed area extends from solid walls, these will form part of the room, too. Brickwork can be painted white for a functional, studio-style effect, or you could clad the walls with painted tongue-and-groove wood panelling, which is neat but mellow – reminiscent of a New England beach-house.

HEAT AND LIGHT

You will probably not have much choice about which direction your conservatory faces and how much sun it gets, but it is worth knowing the difference it will make. Rooms that get year-round sun need good ventilation and shade to avoid heat build-up. Rooms that enjoy afternoon or morning sunlight only are more comfortable, and better for plants which enjoy the indirect light. Rooms that face away from the sun will be fairly bright in summer but without direct sunlight for the rest of year, so will need efficient heating.

- Fit separate heating controls in your conservatory so that you can adjust the temperature independently from the rest of the house.
- Underfloor heating is a good idea, especially as you will not have much wall space to play with.
- Use low-emissivity glass to improve insulation – this allows the heat in but not out.
- Add good ventilation – this is especially important for sunny rooms. Solar-powered air vents are available that will operate automatically when the sun shines.
- Fit blinds to screen glare and prevent the space from overheating. Look out for blinds with a reflective metallic surface to reduce heat build-up during periods of sustained sunshine.
- Add candlelight and atmospheric lamps so that the room can be used in the evening as well as when it is sunlit during the day.

balconies and terraces

In fine weather, the most satisfying way of enjoying more space is to be able to use the outdoors as an extra room. A balcony, terrace or small garden will open up the home and provide an additional sitting or eating area that instantly takes full advantage of the increased light and lack of restriction.

A ground-floor terrace can be laid with stone paving slabs, or with wooden decking tiles for a quicker finish, but with either of these treatments, you may have a step down to the terrace from the adjoining room, creating an undesirable definite divide between the indoors and outdoors.

To establish a more natural link between the two areas, it might be a better idea to build a decking platform – more like a traditional-style veranda – that will sit level with the indoor floor, so that the room appears to extend seamlessly into the open.

DESIGNER DECKING

A platform like this can be built out over a lawn or other surface, giving you a comfortable area of planked wood laid on top of a framework of support beams and joists, which are fixed to posts sunk firmly into the ground. It can be done on a DIY basis (many companies sell the timber and will provide full instructions) and the wood usually comes ready treated to preserve its life (although you will need to treat raw edges yourself where you cut lengths to fit).

left *Timber decking extends this elegant wood-floored sitting room out into the secluded garden, with French doors linking the two areas so that in summer, with the doors wide open, they feel like one huge room.*

The planks themselves can be laid crossways or diagonally to create different effects, so plan your deck area carefully before you buy the wood so that you know precisely how many planks of what sizes you need.

The finished deck can be open-sided, like an apron extending from a stage, which emphasizes the sense of the garden beyond, or you could enclose it with a balustrade or trellis screen, keeping it part of the room that it adjoins.

On upper floors, balconies can be decked with timber to make them feel more 'furnished' than a plain concrete or asphalt floor. Decking panels, usually laid at alternate angles to create a chequerboard effect, are designed with close planks laid on wider-spaced struts, raising the surface off the ground slightly to allow for drainage underneath.

URBAN OPTIONS

Timber creates a mellow but contemporary effect, reminiscent of Oriental gardens and water-front settings. For a cooler, more urban look, a small terrace or balcony can be laid with closely spaced metal grids – not so comfortable to walk on with bare feet, but adding an industrial edge to the soft contours of trees and foliage. Mixing different materials like this – wood and steel, toughened glass and areas of smooth flat pebbles – strikes a modern feel by combining functional strength and natural good looks.

A SEAMLESS DIVIDE

To make the most of the deck effect, aim for doors that open up the back of the house as much as possible, making the wall unobtrusive so that there is little divide between indoors and out. This seamless effect can be created with doors or full-height windows that fold or slide sideways. Sliding doors, based on the simple Japanese screen principle, can be pulled back as far as there is clear wall space to take them. More sophisticated designs have panels that

slide over one another so that they take up less space when pulled back.

Folding doors will draw aside along a track so that the glazed panels stack neatly at the sides. It is the same principle as folding cupboard doors, now being adapted for exterior use so that it creates in effect a folding wall – secure and weatherproof when closed; completely open to the garden when pulled back.

You can fit a full-height sash window that spans the room's width and opens upwards – like a traditional sash but with four or five narrow horizontal sections instead of two – providing a glass wall that can be raised one section at a time, forming a narrow glazed strip at the top.

Disappearing walls like these will need to be cleared by a structural engineer to check that you are not interfering with the structural support of the building, but they will make a massive difference to the feel of the space.

above Natural materials such as slate, stone, wood and terracotta are wonderfully versatile in forging links between indoor and outdoor worlds. Here, a huge sphere of granite has been installed as a fountain so that the water trickles down through layers of slate. The whitewashed wall behind gives the whole setting a slightly Mediterranean feel.

shade and shelter

Balconies, decks and terraces need some sort of cover to protect them from punishing direct sunlight and unseasonable rain. Halfway between an open terrace and a closed conservatory, covered areas make gardens far more usable whatever the weather.

These can provide what is in effect a temporary extension, either attached to the house or free-standing in the garden. The fabric is tough and waterproof as well as an effective shelter from the sun. Go for plain white or cream rather than colourful candy stripes – the impression you want to create is neutral and modern, not beach umbrella. Fixed to the house, an awning can overhang a balcony or terrace, or enclose a walled area or small garden to make it feel more like a room.

Miniature marquees, designed as a canvas cover fitted over a four-legged frame, will provide a free-standing alternative, creating an instant

left The industrial-style ironwork of this balcony structure reinforces its urban setting but also provides a background for climbing plants and potted trees to soften the effect. Timber decking and trelliswork add a more mellow element to the design.

opposite A canvas canopy will provide much-needed shade for small gardens and terraces. Here, it creates the centrepiece for an area of decking enclosed by trellis, railings and traditional brick walls. Keeping the canvas either white or cream maintains the natural effect of other materials in the scheme.

roof for a small garden. Alternatively, you could create your canopy with a sheet of tough sail cloth or canvas tent fabric. Insert metal eyelets in the corners and along the edges, and use stout cord to lash one side of the cloth to metal rings fixed in the house walls. Or use metal clips instead of cord to attach the canopy to the wall – ironmongers sell rings for joining chain links, rather like padlocks. Pull the canopy taut to stop it collecting rain. The eyelets in the outer corners can be attached to rings in nearby walls or slotted on to pointed poles embedded in the garden, similar to tent poles. The result is like a fly-sheet or an open-sided tent.

FRAMEWORK AND FOLIAGE

More permanent structures can be created with frameworks of wood or steel, sometimes in combination with plants to fill in the gaps.

Simple, inexpensive wooden trellis will provide side screens (although not strong enough to lean against, so be careful on roof terraces), or you could build a complete frame to provide overhead beams as well as uprights.

The traditional pergola, a framework over which climbing plants can be trained, will look just as effective on a city balcony as in a garden, but it could be built of steel with mesh sides for a really urban look, reminiscent of a factory walkway. Or you could go for a wooden frame but screen the top with sheets of perspex – a smart modern alternative in the absence of ready-grown climbers.

Plant clematis, vines or runner beans for a homegrown vegetable crop at the foot of the pergola posts and, while you are waiting for them to grow, hang the posts with wall planters or hanging baskets to provide temporary cover.

design options:

AN EXTRA ROOM IN THE GARDEN

● As an alternative to extending your home, you may be able to find space in the garden for a self-contained extra room. Sheds and summerhouses (both available in flatpack form) and decommissioned beach-huts can be kitted out as studies, workrooms, playrooms, alfresco dining rooms and even spare bedrooms. Look for a design that will open right out at the front if you want to use it as a place to sit in good weather or as a summer dining room. Have power (and if necessary telephone) points fitted if you want to install proper lighting or to run office equipment.

● Sheds and summerhouses need to be laid on a level base of brick, concrete or paving stones. Inside, you can lay a floor of insulating foil-covered hardboard as a base for rugs or natural matting. If the room will be solely for summer use, lining the inside walls and roof with fabric will be enough to keep draughts at bay. Use discontinued lines or factory seconds of tough calico or cotton, and fix it in place with a staple gun. For more robust insulation, add thick mineral wool or polystyrene sheets, and draught-proof the windows with perspex sheeting held in place by quadrant edging.

● Paint the wooden exterior so that it coordinates with your house and garden. Use weather-resistant paint or woodstain to help the surface withstand rain and sun-bleaching.

colours

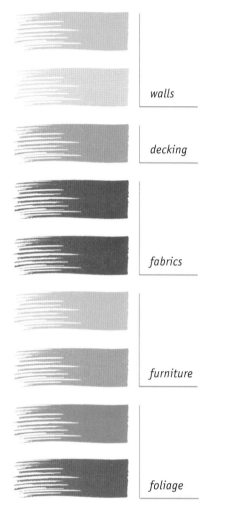

walls

decking

fabrics

furniture

foliage

room recipe:
outdoor living room

Versatile furniture and dramatic structural effects turn this simple concrete shelter into a cool, contemporary-style extension of the house, open to the garden but shaded from the heat of the sun.

WHY IT WORKS:

It's the simplicity of the idea that makes it so effective. Without its furnishings the structure would be no more than a carport, with concrete walls and roof providing basic shelter from the weather. The addition of the slanting, ellipse-shaped windows, however, has two key results: it provides light and views to open up the space and dispel its box-like image, and it contributes a strong design element by accenting both the size of the space and the thickness of the walls. Slicing through the concrete at an angle, these unexpected holes ensure that it looks more like a modern sculpture than a suburban garage.

With the structure in place, the floor provides a contrasting surface in mellow timber decking, softening the overall effect and adding a sense of comfort similar to that of an indoor room. Simple and textured, it has an inviting warmth that brings the space to life and acts as a starting point for the rest of the furnishings. The clever benches are created from steel frames, painted light blue and topped with panels of concrete so that they can act as both seats and tables. Extra seating is supplied by slatted wooden chairs that echo the lines of the flooring, and there are plenty of cushions available to soften the hard edges and make this a comfortable place to sit at any time of day, with the greenery of the garden providing a third wall to complete the room.

KEY INGREDIENTS:

TIMBER FLOORING
Wooden decking underfoot is mellow and comfortable, providing a link with the interior floors of the house and softening the stark functional impression of the concrete walls.

SCULPTURAL STYLE
The unusual oval windows in the walls add a strong sense of modern design that contrasts with the organic world of the garden and gives this extra room its own distinctive architecture.

BENCH SEATING
Neat benches topped with concrete slabs define the space, doubling as both seats and tables with simple cushions in leather and suede added for comfort.

FOLIAGE BACKDROP
Mature trees and shrubs keep the garden enclosed and secluded, giving the uncompromising lines of the solid structure a textured background of shade and greenery.

CANDLELIGHT
Atmospheric lighting makes it a place to sit at night as well as during the day, turning it into an occasional dining room. Candles in garden-planted holders add extra drama along the open side of the space.

index

Page numbers in italic refer to photographs and captions

acknowledgements

BIBLIOGRAPHY

Bird, Julia, *Simple Style* (London: Quadrille, 2001)
Graining, Jane, *Compact Living* (London: Mitchell Beazley London, 1999)
Hanan, Ali (introduction), *Chic Modern* (London: Conran Octopus, 2002)
Hilliard, Elizabeth, *Simple Storage Solutions* (London: Kyle Cathie, 2002)
Niesewand, Nonie, *Contemporary Details* (London: Mitchell Beazley, 1992)
Smith, Susy, *House Beautiful: Small Space Living* (London: Ebury Press, 1993)

AUTHOR'S ACKNOWLEDGEMENTS

With thanks to Roy Ilott for information on planning permission, building regulations and structural issues.

More information on all structural projects and materials is available from The Building Centre, 26 Store Street, London WC1E 7BT

Executive Editor: Doreen Palamartschuk-Gillon

Editor: Jessica Cowie

Executive Art Editor: Peter Burt

Designer: Les Needham

Special Photography: Sebastian Hedgecoe

Picture Researcher: Christine Junemann

Production Controller: Manjit Sihra

PICTURE ACKNOWLEDGEMENTS

Abode/Neil Davies 118/Andreas Einsiedel 162 /Tony Hall 96, 168, 181/Tim Inrie 43 top, 61, 123 /Bernard O'Sullivan 97, 129, 164, 177, 184/Ian Perry 142/Brett Prestige 107/Trevor Richards 93, 130, 159, 180/Simon Whitmore 29 right, 95, 157 right /Tim Young 21, 38 left, 56, 116, 117, 160

Etienne Clement, Jones Wood Architects 22

Crown Paints 25, 39

Wilma Interiors (Stockists tel: 0800 581 984, www.wilman.co.uk) 24

Elizabeth Whiting Associates 59 left, 171 bottom /Jon Bouchier 19/Mike Crockett 74, 150, 154 /Rodney Hyett 103/Lu Jeffery 18, 27, 153 /Tom Leighton 75, 80/Di Lewis 69/Neil Lorimer 60, 99 bottom/Mark Luscombe-Whyte 47, 66 /Mark Nicholson 173/Michael Nicholson 16 /Spike Powell 70, 146/Tim Street-Porter 36, 134 /Mark Thomas 144, 157 left

Fired Earth (Stockists tel: 01295 814300, www.firedearth.com) 136, 137 top

Octopus Publishing Group Ltd/Michael Banks 166 /Dominic Blackmore 58, 111 left, 163, 169 /Graham Dixon 10, 12/Sebastian Hedgecoe, architects: Littman Goddard Hogarth Ltd. (tel:020 7351 7871, www.lgh-architects.co.uk) 15, 48, 102, 119, 137 bottom, 152, architects: Yoo Ltd (tel: 020 7009 0100, www.yooarehere.com) 30, 35, 41, 82, 108, 140, Roger Black Development, agent: FPD Savills Int. (tel: 020 7531 2500, www.stepneycity.com) 7, 79, 110, 111 right, 138, 139, 141 top, 182, 183 /Tom Mannion 14, 31 top, 54, 99 top, 101 top, 112, 170 /Neil Mersh 88/Peter Myers 28, 31 bottom, 33, 43 bottom, 98, 101 bottom, 124, 133, 135, Gunnar Orefelt Architects 73/Simon Upton 63, 92, 171 top /David Wainwright 13 bottom

The Holding Company (Stockists tel: 020 8445 2888, www.theholdingcompany.co.uk) 13 top, 81, 85 left, 85 right, 156

Homebase 147 left, 147 right, 148

The Interior Archive/Tim Baddow, designer: de Taillac 87, 121/Fritz von der Schulenburg, architect: Nico Rensch 120, designer: John Stefanidis 11/Simon Upton 165/Luke White, designer: Caroline Gardener 149/Edina van der Wyck, architect: Richard Rogers 51, designer: Atlanta Bartlett 52

Cath Kidston/Pia Tryde (Stockists tel: 0207 221 4000, Kath Kidson Ltd, 8 Clarenden Cross, London W11 4PE) 44

Ray Main/Mainstream 20, 26, 34, 49 left, 62, 84, 115, 128, 132, designer: Dermert Gavin 186

Narratives/Jan Baldwin 46, 53, 59 right, 83, 105 architects: Melloco&Moore 67, architects: Mullman Seidman 78, architect: Pierre Lombart 32, architect: Richard Rogers 64, 94, designer: Alistair Hendy 114, designer: Bill Ambers 100, designer: Camilla Ridley 42, designer: Charlotte Crosland 37, MMM Architects (tel: 020 7286 9499) 8, 57, Jonathan Clark (tel; 020 7286 5676) 72, 126/Tamsyn Hill 113, architect: Hans-Peter Obwaller 50, 131 /Brian Leonard, architect: Terry Dorrough 49 right, 176/Polly Wreford 29 left, 40, 76, 141 bottom

Andrew Pilkington Architect (tel: 020 7351 0060, www.andrewpilkington.com) 2, 38 right, 104, 179

Red Cover/Graham Atkins-Hughs 90/Jon Bouchier 155/James Mitchell, designer: Stephen Woodham 185/Ed Reeve, architect: Misha Stefan 6 /Verity Welstead 65, 178

Retna UK/Lucinda Symons/House Beautiful UK 151

Theis+Kahn Architects (tel: 020 7729 9329, www.theisandkahn.com)/Nicholas Kane 167, 174 /Nick Pope 17